The Politics of Anti-Semitism

CounterPunch

The Politics of Anti-Semitism

Edited by
Alexander Cockburn
and Jeffrey St. Clair

AK PRESS
EDINBURGH · LONDON · OAKLAND

CounterPunch

Petrolia

First published by
CounterPunch and AK Press 2003
© CounterPunch 2003

CounterPunch
PO Box 228 Petrolia, California, 95558

AK Press
674A 23rd St, Oakland, California 94612-1163
www.akpress.org

PO Box 12766, Edinburgh, Scotland EH89YE
www.akuk.com

ISBN   1-90259-377-4

Library of Congress Cataloguing in-Publication data

A catalog record for this book is available from the Library of
Congress

Typeset in Tyfa and Stainless
Printed and bound in Canada

Designed by Tiffany Wardle

Contents

Introduction

T HERE'S NO MORE EXPLOSIVE TOPIC IN AMERICAN PUBLIC
life today than the issue of Israel, its treatment of
Palestinians and its influence on American politics. Yet
the topic is one that is so hedged with anxiety, fury and fear that
honest discussion is often impossible.

Our aim in *The Politics of Anti-Semitism* is to lift this embargo.
We try to breach the blockade from a number of different direc-
tions.

Apologists for Israel's repression of Palestinians toss the
word "anti-Semite" at any critic of what Zionism has meant in
practice for Palestinians on the receiving end. So some of the
essays in this book address the issue of what constitutes genuine
anti-Semitism—Jew-hatred—as opposed to disingenuous, specious charges of "anti-Semitism" hurled at rational appraisals of
the state of Israel's political, military and social conduct.

We offer first-hand accounts (those of Robert Fisk and
Norman Finkelstein for example) of just how malignly or comi-
cally lunatic the "anti-Semite" baiting can be.

There is in the US a broad political culture of opposition to
Israel's conduct and to the US role in sponsoring it with political, military and budgetary muscle. We offer ground-zero
accounts by those who have been part of that opposition.

After 9/11 it became apparent to many that Sharon's government was exploiting the new political terrain to further its own
objectives, and that senior members of the US government had
long career histories as promoters of the Israeli interest in
Washington. The essays by Sunderland and the Christisons
cover this issue of dual loyalty.

So powerful is the Israel lobby that it was even able to bury a
US congressional investigation into the deliberate attack on the
USS Liberty by the Israeli Air Force in 1967, an attack that left

34 US sailors dead and 172 wounded. Jeffrey St Clair recalls this astounding demonstration of the clout of the Israel lobby in official Washington.

The bottom line is Israel's denial of Palestinians' right to a nation, living within secure borders, just like Israeli Jews. Many of the contributors to this book have borne witness to the savagery of that denial, and have been duly attacked with the venom of the "anti-Semite!" insult. Just how awful the occupation is, and how cruel the onslaughts on the Intifada, is eloquently described by a Palestinian, Edward Said, and an Israeli Jew, Yigal Bronner. Both, please note, still nourish a vision of a future in which Israeli Jews and Palestinians live peacefully, side by side.

These essays, half of them by Jews, have appeared either in the pages of our newsletter, CounterPunch, or on our website, WWW.COUNTERPUNCH.ORG.

Alexander Cockburn / Jeffrey St. Clair

Michael Neumann
What Is Anti-Semitism?

EVERY ONCE IN A WHILE, SOME LEFT-WING JEWISH WRITER will take a deep breath, open up his (or her) great big heart, and tell us that criticism of Israel or Zionism is not anti-Semitism. Silently they congratulate themselves on their courage. With a little sigh, they suppress any twinge of concern that maybe the goyim—let alone the Arabs—can't be trusted with this dangerous knowledge.

Sometimes it is gentile hangers-on, whose ethos if not their identity aspires to Jewishness, who take on this task. Not to be utterly risque, they then hasten to remind us that anti-Semitism is nevertheless to be taken very seriously. That Israel, backed by a pronounced majority of Jews, happens to be waging a race war against the Palestinians is all the more reason we should be on our guard. Who knows, it might possibly stir up some resentment!

I take a different view. I think we should almost never take anti-Semitism seriously, and maybe we should have some fun with it. I think it is particularly unimportant to the Israel-Palestine conflict, except perhaps as a diversion from the real issues. I will argue for the truth of these claims; I also defend their propriety. I don't think making them is on a par with pulling the wings off flies.

'Anti-Semitism', properly and narrowly speaking, doesn't mean hatred of Semites; that is to confuse etymology with definition. It means hatred of Jews. But here, immediately, we come up against the venerable shell-game of Jewish identity: "Look! We're a religion! No! a race! No! a cultural entity! Sorry—a religion!" When we tire of this game, we get suckered into another: "Anti-Zionism is anti-Semitism!" quickly alternates with "Don't confuse Zionism with Judaism! How dare you, you anti-Semite!"

Well, let's be good sports. Let's try defining 'anti-Semitism' as broadly as any supporter of Israel would ever want: anti-Semitism can be hatred of the Jewish race, or culture, or religion, or hatred of Zionism. Hatred, or dislike, or opposition, or slight unfriendliness.

But supporters of Israel won't find this game as much fun as they expect. Inflating the meaning of 'anti-Semitism' to include anything politically damaging to Israel is a double-edged sword. It may be handy for smiting your enemies, but the problem is that definitional inflation, like any inflation, cheapens the currency. The more things get to count as anti-Semitic, the less awful anti-Semitism is going to sound. This happens because, while no one can stop you from inflating definitions, you still don't control the facts. In particular, no definition of 'anti-Semitism' is going to eradicate the substantially pro-Palestinian version of the facts that I espouse, as do most people in Europe, a great many Israelis and a growing number of North Americans.

What difference does that make? Suppose, for example, an Israeli rightist says that the settlements represent the pursuit of aspirations fundamental to the Jewish people, and to oppose the settlements is anti-Semitism. We might have to accept this claim; certainly it is difficult to refute. But we also cannot abandon the well-founded belief that the settlements strangle the Palestinian people and extinguish any hope of peace. So definitional acrobatics are all for nothing: we can only say, Screw the fundamental aspirations of the Jewish people; the settlements are wrong. We must add that since we are obliged to oppose the settlements, we are obliged to be anti-Semitic. Through definitional inflation, some form of anti-Semitism becomes morally obligatory.

It gets worse if anti-Zionism is labeled anti-Semitic, because the settlements, even if they do not represent fundamental aspirations of the Jewish people, are an entirely plausible extension of Zionism. To oppose them is indeed to be anti-Zionist, and therefore, by the stretched definition, anti-Semitic. The more anti-Semitism expands to include opposition to Israeli policies, the better it looks. Given the crimes to be laid at the feet of Zionism, there is another simple syllogism: anti-Zionism is a moral obligation, so, if anti-Zionism is anti-Semitism, anti-Semitism is a moral obligation.

What crimes? Even most apologists for Israel have given up denying them, and merely hint that noticing them is a bit anti-Semitic. After all, Israel "is no worse than anyone else". First, so what? At age six we knew that "everyone's doing it" is no excuse; have we forgotten? Second, the crimes are no worse only when divorced from their purpose. Yes, other people have killed civilians, watched them die for want of medical care, destroyed their homes, ruined their crops and used them as human shields. But Israel does these things to correct the inaccuracy of Israel Zangwill's 1901 assertion that "Palestine is a country without a people; the Jews are a people without a country". It hopes to create a land entirely empty of gentiles, an Arabia deserta in which Jewish children can laugh and play throughout a wasteland called peace.

Well before the Hitler era, Zionists came thousands of miles to dispossess people who had never done them the slightest harm, and whose very existence they contrived to ignore. Zionist atrocities were not part of the initial plan. They emerged as the racist obliviousness of a persecuted people blossomed into the racial supremacist ideology of a persecuting one. That is why the commanders who directed the rapes, mutilations and child-killings of Deir Yassin went on to become prime ministers of Israel. But these murders were not enough. Today, when Israel could have peace for the taking, it conducts another round of dispossession, slowly, deliberately making Palestine unliveable for Palestinians, and liveable for Jews. Its purpose is not defense or public order but the extinction of a people. True,

Israel has enough PR-savvy to eliminate them with an American rather than a Hitlerian level of violence. This is a kinder, gentler genocide that portrays its perpetrators as victims.

Israel is building a racial state, not a religious one. Like my parents, I have always been an atheist. I am entitled by the biology of my birth to Israeli citizenship; you, perhaps, are the most fervent believer in Judaism but are not so entitled. Palestinians are being squeezed and killed for me, not for you. They are to be forced into Jordan, to perish in a civil war. So no, shooting Palestinian civilians is not like shooting Vietnamese or Chechen civilians. The Palestinians aren't "collateral damage" in a war against well-armed communist or separatist forces. They are being shot because Israel thinks all Palestinians should vanish or die, so people with one Jewish grandparent can build subdivisions on the rubble of their homes. This is not the bloody mistake of a blundering superpower but an emerging evil, the deliberate strategy of a state conceived in and dedicated to an increasingly vicious ethnic nationalism. It has relatively few corpses to its credit so far, but its nuclear weapons can kill perhaps 25 million people in a few hours.

Do we want to say it is anti-Semitic to accuse not just the Israelis but Jews generally of complicity in these crimes against humanity? Again, maybe not, because there is a quite reasonable case for such assertions. Compare them, for example, to the claim that Germans generally were complicit in such crimes. This never meant that every last German, man, woman, idiot and child, was guilty. It meant that most Germans were. Their guilt, of course, did not consist in shoving naked prisoners into gas chambers. It consisted in support for the people who planned such acts, or—as many overwrought, moralistic Jewish texts will tell you—for denying the horror unfolding around them, for failing to speak out and resist, for passive consent. Note that the extreme danger of any kind of active resistance is not supposed to be an excuse here.

Well, virtually no Jew is in any kind of danger from speaking out. And speaking out is the only sort of resistance required. If many Jews spoke out, it would have an enormous effect. But the overwhelming majority of Jews do not, and in the vast majority of cases, this is because they support Israel. Now perhaps the whole notion of collective responsibility should be discarded; perhaps some clever person will convince us that we have to do this. But at present, the case for Jewish complicity seems much stronger than the case for German complicity. So, if it is not racist or unreasonable to say that the Germans were complicit in crimes against humanity, then it is neither racist nor unreasonable to say the same of the Jews. And should the notion of collective responsibility be discarded, it would still be reasonable to say that many, perhaps most, Jewish adults support a state that commits war crimes, because that's just true. So if saying these things is anti-Semitic, than it can be reasonable to be anti-Semitic.

In other words, there is a choice to be made. You can use 'anti-Semitism' to fit your political agenda, or you can use it as a term of condemnation, but you can't do both. If anti-Semitism is to stop coming out reasonable or moral, it has to be narrowly and unpolemically defined. It would be safe to confine anti-Semitism to explicitly racial hatred of Jews, to attacking people simply because they had been born Jewish. But it would be uselessly safe: even the Nazis did not claim to hate people simply because they had been born Jewish. They claimed to hate the Jews because they were out to dominate the Aryans. Clearly such a view should count as anti-Semitic, whether it belongs to the cynical racists who concocted it or to the fools who swallowed it.

There is only one way to guarantee that the term 'anti-Semitism' captures only bad acts or attitudes towards Jews. We have to start with what we can all agree are of that sort, and see that the term names all and only them. We probably share enough morality to do this.

For instance, we share enough morality to say that all racially based acts and hatreds are bad, so we can safely count them as anti-Semitic. But not all 'hostility towards Jews', even if that means hostility towards the overwhelming majority of Jews, should count as anti-Semitic. By the same token, nor should all hostility towards Judaism, or Jewish culture.

I, for example, grew up in Jewish culture and, like many people growing up in a culture, I have come to dislike it. But it is unwise to count my dislike as anti-Semitic, not because I am Jewish but because it is harmless. Perhaps not utterly harmless; maybe, to some tiny extent, it will somehow encourage some of the harmful acts or attitudes we'd want to call anti-Semitic. But so what? Exaggerated philo-Semitism, which regards all Jews as brilliant warm and witty saints, might have the same effect. The dangers posed by my dislike are much too small to matter. Even widespread, collective loathing for a culture is normally harmless. French culture, for instance, seems to be widely disliked in North America, and no one, including the French, consider this some sort of racial crime.

Not even all acts and attitudes harmful to Jews generally should be considered anti-Semitic. Many people dislike American culture; some boycott American goods. Both the attitude and the acts may harm Americans generally, but there is nothing morally objectionable about either. Defining these acts as anti-Americanism will only mean that some anti-Americanism is perfectly acceptable. If you call opposition to Israeli policies anti-Semitic on the grounds that this opposition harms Jews generally, it will only mean that some anti-Semitism is equally acceptable.

If anti-Semitism is going to be a term of condemnation, then, it must apply beyond explicitly racist acts or thoughts or feelings. But it cannot apply beyond clearly unjustified and serious hostility to Jews. The Nazis made up historical fantasies to justify their attacks; so do modern anti-Semites who trust in the *Protocols of the Elders of Zion.* So do the closet racists who complain about Jewish dominance of the economy. This is anti-Semitism in a narrow, negative sense of the word. It is action or propaganda designed to hurt Jews, not because of anything they could avoid doing but because they are what they are. It also applies to the attitudes that propaganda tries to instill. Though not always explicitly racist, it involves racist motives and the intention to do real damage. Reasonably well-founded opposition to Israeli policies, even if that opposition hurts all Jews, does not fit this description. Neither does simple, harmless dislike of things Jewish.

So far, I've suggested that it's best to narrow the definition of 'anti-Semitism' so that no act can be both anti-Semitic and unobjectionable. But we can go further. Now that we're through playing games, let's ask about the role of genuine, bad anti-Semitism in the Israel-Palestine conflict, and in the world at large.

Undoubtedly there is genuine anti-Semitism in the Arab world: the distribution of the *Protocols of the Elders of Zion,* the myths about stealing the blood of gentile babies. This is utterly inexcusable. So was your failure to answer Aunt Bee's last letter. In other words, it is one thing to be told, "You must simply accept that anti-Semitism is evil; to do otherwise is to put yourself outside our moral world". But it is quite something else to have someone try to bully you into proclaiming that anti-Semitism is the Evil of Evils. We are not children learning morality; it is our responsibility to set our own moral priorities. We cannot do this by looking at horrible images from 1945 or listening to the anguished cries of suffering columnists. We have to ask how much harm anti-Semitism is doing, or is likely to do, not in the past but today. And we must ask where such harm might occur, and why.

Supposedly there is great danger in the anti-Semitism of the Arab world. But Arab anti-Semitism isn't the cause of Arab hostility towards Israel or even towards Jews. It is an effect. The progress of Arab anti-Semitism fits nicely with the progress of Jewish encroachment and Jewish atrocities. This is not to excuse genuine anti-Semitism; it is to trivialize it. It came to the Middle East with Zionism and it will abate when Zionism ceases to be an expansionist threat. Indeed its chief cause is not anti-Semitic propaganda but the decades' old, systematic and unrelenting efforts of Israel to implicate all Jews in its crimes. If Arab anti-Semitism persists after a peace agreement, we can all get together and cluck about it. But it still won't do Jews much actual harm. Arab governments could only lose by permitting attacks on their Jewish citizens; to do so would invite Israeli intervention. And there is little reason to expect such attacks to materialize: if all the horrors of Israel's recent campaigns did not provoke them, it is hard to imagine what would. It would probably take some Israeli act so awful and so criminal as to overshadow the attacks themselves.

If anti-Semitism is likely to have terrible effects, it is far more likely to have them in Western Europe. The neo-fascist resurgence there is all too real. But is it a danger to Jews? There is no doubt that LePen, for instance, is anti-Semitic. There is also no evidence whatever that he intends to do anything about it. On the contrary, he makes every effort to pacify the Jews, and perhaps even enlist their help against his real targets, the "Arabs". He would hardly be the first political figure to ally himself with people he dislikes. But if he had some deeply hidden plan against the Jews, that *would* be unusual: Hitler and the Russian anti-Semitic rioters were wonderfully open about their intentions, and they didn't court Jewish support. And it is a fact that some French Jews see LePen as a positive development or even an ally. (See, for instance, "'LePen is good for us,'

Jewish supporter says", Ha'aretz, May 4, 2002, and Mr. Goldenburg's April 23rd comments on France TV.)

Of course, there are historical reasons for fearing a horrendous attack on Jews. And anything is possible: there could be a massacre of Jews in Paris tomorrow, or of Algerians. Which is more likely? If there are any lessons of history, they must apply in roughly similar circumstances. Europe today bears very little resemblance to Europe in 1933. And there are positive possibilities as well: why is the likelihood of a pogrom greater than the likelihood that anti-Semitism will fade into ineffectual nastiness? Any legitimate worries must rest on some evidence that there really is a threat.

The incidence of anti-Semitic attacks might provide such evidence. But this evidence is consistently fudged: no distinction is made between attacks against Jewish monuments and symbols as opposed to actual attacks against Jews. In addition, so much is made of an increase in the frequency of attacks that the very low absolute level of attacks escapes attention. The symbolic attacks have indeed increased to significant absolute numbers. The physical attacks have not.(*) More important, most of these attacks are by Muslim residents: in other words, they come from a widely hated, vigorously policed and persecuted minority who don't stand the slightest chance of undertaking a serious campaign of violence against Jews.

It is very unpleasant that roughly half a dozen Jews have been hospitalized—none killed—due to recent attacks across Europe. But anyone who makes this into one of the world's important problems simply hasn't looked at the world. These attacks are a matter for the police, not a reason for us to police ourselves and others to counter some deadly spiritual disease. That sort of reaction is appropriate only when racist attacks occur in societies indifferent or hostile to the minority attacked. Those who really care about recurrent Nazism, for instance, should save their anguished concern for the far bloodier, far more widely condoned attacks on gypsies, whose history of persecution is fully comparable to the Jewish past. The position of Jews is much closer to the position of whites, who are also, of course, the victims of racist attacks.

No doubt many people reject this sort of cold-blooded calculation. They will say that, with the past looming over us, even one anti-Semitic slur is a terrible thing, and its ugliness is not to be measured by a body count. But if we take a broader view of the matter, anti-Semitism becomes less, not more important. To regard any shedding of Jewish blood as a world-shattering calamity, one that defies all measurement and comparison, is racism, pure and simple; the valuing of one race's blood over all others. The fact that Jews have been persecuted for centuries and suffered terribly half a century ago doesn't wipe out the fact that in Europe today Jews are insiders with far less to suffer and fear than many other ethnic groups. Certainly racist attacks against a well-off minority are just as evil as racist attacks against a poor and powerless minority. But equally evil attackers do not make for equally worrisome attacks.

It is not Jews who live most in the shadow of the concentration camp. LePen's "transit camps" are for "Arabs", not Jews. And though there are politically significant parties containing many anti-Semites, not one of those parties shows any sign of articulating, much less implementing, an anti-Semitic agenda. Nor is there any particular reason to suppose that, once in power, they would change their tune. Haider's Austria is not considered dangerous for Jews; neither was Tudjman's Croatia. And were there to be such danger, well, a nuclear-armed Jewish state stands ready to welcome any refugees, as do the US and Canada. And to say there are no real dangers now is not to say that we should ignore any dangers that may arise. If in France, for instance, the Front National starts advocating transit camps for Jews, or institutes anti-Jewish immigration policies, then we should be alarmed. But we should not be alarmed that something alarming might just conceivably happen; there are far more alarming things going on than that!

One might reply that if things are not more alarming, it is only because the Jews and others have been so vigilant in combatting anti-Semitism. But this isn't plausible. For one thing, vigilance about anti-Semitism is a kind of tunnel vision: as neofascists are learning, they can escape notice by keeping quiet about Jews. For another, there has been no great danger to Jews even in traditionally anti-Semitic countries where the world is *not* vigilant, like Croatia or the Ukraine. Countries that get very little attention seem no more dangerous than countries that get a lot. As for the vigorous reaction to LePen in France, that seems to have a lot more to do with French revulsion at neofascism than with the scoldings of the Anti-Defamation League. To suppose that the Jewish organizations and earnest columnists who pounce on anti-Semitism are saving the world from disaster is like claiming that Bertrand Russell and the Quakers were all that saved us from nuclear war.

Now, one might say, "whatever the real dangers, these events are truly agonizing for Jews, and bring back unbearably painful memories". That may be true for the very few who still have those memories; it is not true for Jews in general. I am a German Jew, and have a good claim to second-generation, third-hand victimhood. Anti-Semitic incidents and a climate of rising anti-Semitism don't really bother me a hell of a lot. I'm much more scared of really dangerous situations, like driving. Besides, even painful memories and anxieties do not carry much weight against the actual physical suffering inflicted by discrimination against many non-Jews.

This is not to belittle all anti-Semitism, everywhere. One often hears of vicious anti-Semites in Poland and Russia, both on the streets and in government. But alarming as that may be, it is also immune to the influence of Israel-Palestine conflicts, and those conflicts are wildly unlikely to affect it one way or another.

Moreover, so far as I know, nowhere is there as much violence against Jews as there is against "Arabs". So even if anti-Semitism is, somewhere, a catastrophically serious matter, we can only conclude that anti-Arab sentiment is far more serious still. And since almost every anti-Semitic group is to a far greater extent anti-immigrant and anti-Arab, these groups can be fought not in the name of anti-Semitism but in the defense of Arabs and immigrants. The anti-Semitic threat posed by these groups shouldn't even make us want to focus on anti-Semitism: they are just as well fought in the name of justice for Arabs and immigrants.

In short, the scandal today is not anti-Semitism but the importance it is given. Israel has committed war crimes. It has implicated Jews generally in these crimes, and Jews generally have hastened to implicate themselves. This has provoked hatred against Jews. Why not? Some of this hatred is racist, some isn't, but who cares? Why should we pay any attention to this issue at all? Is it of any importance that Israel's race war has provoked bitter anger when we compare that anger with the war itself? Is the remote possibility that somewhere, sometime, somehow, this hatred may in theory, possibly kill some Jews of any importance next to the brutal, actual, physical persecution of Palestinians, and the hundreds of thousands of votes for Arabs to be herded into transit camps? Oh, but I forgot. Drop everything. Someone spray-painted anti-Semitic slogans on a synagogue.

* Not even the ADL and B'nai B'rith include attacks on Israel in the tally; they speak of "The insidious way we have seen the conflict between Israelis and Palestinians used by anti-Semites". And like many other people, I don't count terrorist attacks by such as Al Qaeda as instances of anti-Semitism but rather of some misdirected quasi-military campaign against the US and Israel. Even if you count them in, it does not seem very dangerous to be a Jew outside Israel.

Michael Neumann is a professor of philosophy at Trent University in Ontario, Canada, and the author of What's Left: Radical Politics and the Radical Psyche.

Scott Handleman
Trivializing Jew-Hatred

PARTISANS OF ISRAEL OFTEN MAKE FALSE ACCUSATIONS OF anti-Semitism to silence Israel's critics. The "anti-Semite!" libel is harmful not only because it censors debate about Israel's racism and human rights abuses but because it trivializes the ugly history of Jew-hatred. A book published in 2002, *Anti-Semitism: Myth and Hate from Antiquity to the Present* (Palgrave Macmillan), documents anti-Semitic myth and its extraordinary human costs. Unfortunately, *Anti-Semitism*, written by history professors Marvin Perry and Frederick Schweitzer, exemplifies the "strongly polemical and apologetical bias" that Hannah Arendt once perceived in Jewish historians of anti-Semitism. In particular, Perry and Schweitzer subscribe to the myth of the uniquely ineradicable quality of Jew-hatred, and to the related notion that all criticism of Jews as Jews is illegitimate anti-Semitism. As I read line after hand-wringing line about the unparalleled badness of anti-Semitism, I felt transported to the Miami Beach of my childhood, trudging in a suit to some Holocaust commemoration or Netanyahu speech with my grandfather, Joe Handleman, a philanthropic pillar of the Jewish community.

Anti-Semitism, a form of racism originating in the nineteenth century, flowered in the rich soils of Christian anti-Judaism: the gospel tale that Jews were Christ-killers. Matthew 27:24-25 reports that "Pilate ... washed his hands in full view of the people, saying, 'My hands are clean of this man's blood; see to that yourselves.' And with one voice all the people cried, 'His blood be upon us, and upon our children'." To Perry and Schweitzer, the singularity of the deicide charge is the golden key that accounts for the assertedly exceptional nature of Jewish maltreatment: "No other religious tradition has condemned a people as the murderers of its god, a unique accusation that has resulted in a unique history of hatred, fear, and persecution." Perhaps for that reason they devote a chapter to the implausibilities and contradictions of the Passion narrative to the extent that it tends to incriminate Jews. Perry and Schweitzer make a spirited argument that the Romans were the real Christ-killers, and that the gospel authors fingered Jews in order to curry favor with the Empire.

The Middle Ages gave birth to a myth that Jews kidnapped and murdered Christian children, using their blood to make Passover matzoh. Jews were also accused of desecrating the host: stealing communion wafers and gleefully profaning the wafer/body of Christ. A third myth held that Jews caused the bubonic plague, by poisoning wells. Down the centuries, both church and state profited from the ritual-murder and host-desecration libels, which led to mass expulsions and the slaughter of tens or hundreds of thousands of Jews. After Jews allegedly kidnapped and crucified Little St. Hugh of Lincoln (having first fattened him with white bread and milk), eighteen Jews were hanged, and King Henry III plundered their property. Churches profited from shrines to martyred Christian children and miraculous bleeding hosts. Two thirteenth-century popes, Innocent IV and Gregory X, denounced the blood libel as a lie; but in 1840, Pope Gregory XVI supported a ritual-murder charge against the Jews of Damascus, and at the end of the nineteenth century, Pope Leo XIII or his representatives stated that "ritual murder is a historical certainty". In 1913, after a boy's mutilated corpse was found near Kiev, high czarist officials, hoping to foment anti-Semitism, conspired with local authorities to charge Mendel Beilis with ritual murder. Prosecutors bribed a witness, but a jury of commoners acquitted Beilis. In 1972, King Faisal of Saudi Arabia said that "while I was in Paris on a visit, the police discovered five murdered children. Their blood had been drained, and it turned out that some Jews had murdered them in order to take their blood and mix it with the bread they eat on that day".

In the nineteenth century, with the invention of race, modern anti-Semitism emerged (although it had anachronistic precedent in medieval Spaniards' prejudice against *conversos*). Conforming their ideology to the social-Darwinist spirit of the times, anti-Semites now hated Jews because of ancestry, not religious practice. Perry and Schweitzer assign the proliferation of modern anti-Semitism to the work of "landholding aristocrats, generals, and clergy, often joined by business and industrial magnates", who used Jew-hating nationalism as a demagogic weapon. (Arendt makes the opposite argument, that anti-Semitism blossomed as the Jews' power declined with the power of the nation-state; left with wealth but not power, they became prime targets for persecution.) In the *Protocols of the Learned Elders of Zion*, for example, anti-Semites famously scapegoated Jews as a shifty class of international conspirators plotting against the gentile nations for world domination by controlling banks and stock exchanges and simultaneously promoting socialism. After the Bible, the Protocols was the world's most widely circulated book between 1918 and 1939. Henry Ford quoted from the Protocols in his International Jew. (Hitler called Ford a great man for standing up to the Jews. In 1938 Ford accepted the Grand Cross of the German Eagle; in 1939, he sent Hitler 50,000 marks as a birthday gift.)

Existing alongside both Christian and secular anti-Semitism has been the stereotype of the Jew as money-grubbing Shylock. The Jews of medieval Europe, excluded from land ownership and crafts, became peddlers, an occupation that Christians then viewed as financially unrewarding and morally suspect. Around 1100, as commerce became lucrative and therefore respectable, Christians forced Jews out of trade, so Jews turned to the emerging field of finance, barred to the Christians by the Bible's prohibition on usury. Over the next few hundred years, Jews became bankers and financiers to the rulers of Europe. By the mid-nineteenth century, for example, Jews, who were 1 percent of Germany's population, generated one-fifth of German economic activity. And a Nazi document cited by Perry and Schweitzer reports that out of 147 members of the stock, produce and metal exchanges in 1933, 116 were Jews. On the other hand, even as Jews swelled the ranks of the rich and middle classes, a majority of European Jews remained poor, particularly in Eastern Europe. Even in Vienna, two-thirds of Jews were destitute in 1880.

Perry and Schweitzer spend a chapter debunking the stereotype of Jew as innate conniving materialist, pointing out that the Torah and Talmud condemn mindless accumulation and commend charity. They explain the historical forces that relegated Jews to the fields of banking and finance. In the sole passage of the book that treats anti-Semitism as a historically comparable phenomenon, they relay Braudel's observation that Europe's Jews constituted a diaspora civilization like the Armenians in the Ottoman Empire, the ethnic Chinese in Indonesia, or the Indians in Uganda, each of which groups came to dominate commerce in their respective areas, earning them enmity as "unduly privileged and prosperous" minority classes, and leading to doom in each case.

But in mentioning how the spectacle of Jewish wealth created resentment and contributed to the flourishing of anti-Semitism in the period leading up to Hitler, Perry and Schweitzer treat Jews not as the partial agents of their own unpopularity but as blameless scapegoats, irrationally targeted by the ever-lurking anti-Semites. Throughout their book, they effectively promote the notion that anti-Semitism has been eternal (at least since the gospels), a notion Hannah Arendt denounced in The Origins of Totalitarianism:

"In view of the final catastrophe, which brought the Jews so near to complete annihilation, the thesis of eternal anti-

Semitism has become more dangerous than ever…. this explanation of anti-Semitism, like the scapegoat theory and for similar reasons, has outlived its refutation by reality….

"It is quite remarkable that the only two doctrines which at least attempt to explain the political significance of the anti-Semitic movement deny all specific Jewish responsibility and refuse to discuss matters in specific historical terms. In this inherent negation of the significance of human behavior, they bear a terrible resemblance to those modern practices and forms of government which, by means of arbitrary terror, liquidate the very possibility of human activity."

Arendt inquired into the origins of modern anti-Semitism by looking at the modern historical functions of the Jew. She found the role of court Jews to be decisive. Jewish bankers allied themselves with whatever regime held power: "It took the French Rothschilds in 1848 hardly twenty-four hours to transfer their services from the government of Louis Philippe to the new short-lived French Republic and again to Napoleon III…. In Germany this sudden and easy change was symbolized, after the revolution of 1918, in the financial policies of the Warburgs on one hand and the shifting political ambitions of Walter Rathenau on the other." Thus, "each class of society which came into a conflict with the state as such became anti-Semitic because the only social group which seemed to represent the state were the Jews".

In Arendt's day, the theoreticians of eternal Jew-hatred hadn't needed to confront the postwar decline in anti-Semitism, since the war was a recent phenomenon and they might be forgiven for thinking the vile prejudice would soon resurface. By contrast, Perry and Schweitzer have to grapple with the fact that anti-Semitism has fallen into disrepute since the Holocaust. They mention a 1998 ADL finding of significantly reduced anti-Semitism in the United States. Frantically hunting for twenty-first century anti-Semites, Perry and Schweitzer ultimately range through the marginal turf of Holocaust deniers and the Nation of Islam, but not before stalking a more popular beast:

"the exacerbation of the Arab-Israeli conflict has generated a resurgence of anti-Semitism in Europe, even among polite circles…. In demonstrations held in many European cities in support of the Palestinians, Israelis were equated with Nazis, Prime Minister Ariel Sharon with Hitler, and the Israeli flag was burned….

"What is most distressing is the way the press and intellectuals, who previously glossed over the Israeli casualties of suicide bombers, were quick to condemn Israel, often sinking into the ordure of anti-Semitism…. Accepting as true the grotesque Palestinian fabrication that a massacre had taken place at Jenin, the press in several countries accused the Israeli army of engaging in genocide."

Thus do Perry and Schweitzer obliviate the massacre victims of Jenin with a method they impute to the hateful Holocaust deniers. (*"Chronicles written by Jews … are disqualified as evidence."*)

Putting aside the Jenin comment and assuming as we must that Perry and Schweitzer were the deluded victims of some crackpot occupation revisionist, their equation of anti-Semitism with criticism of Israel is typical of the reasoning of many American Jews, including a few personages who have the *chutzpah* to speak in all of our names. The premise of eternal anti-Semitism holds that Jews are forever the targets of irrational hatred: the collective behavior of Jews cannot influence its course. A corollary idea, popular in recent decades, holds that a strong Israel is necessary to safeguard world Jewry. And when people criticize Israel's policies and practices, it can be deduced that they are only the latest in the protean historical chain of Jew-haters, confirming the thesis of eternal anti-Semitism.

A neat circle of logic. Arendt saw that "the only possible movement in the realm of logic is the process of deduction from a premise…. Ideologies always assume that one idea is sufficient to explain everything ... and that no experience can teach any-thing because everything is comprehended in this consistent process of logical deduction.... Once it has established its premise, its point of departure, experiences no longer interfere with ideological thinking, nor can it be taught by reality". The very heart of totalitarianism is the fear of self-contradiction that compels us to follow the chain of deductions—hence Hitler's "ice cold reasoning", Stalin's dialectic, military commands in the West Bank. The inner capacity for freedom is the capacity to think outside the chain: "Over the beginning, no logic, no cogent deduction can have any power, because its chain presup-poses, in the form of a premise, the beginning. As terror is needed lest with the birth of each new human being a new beginning arise and raise its voice in the world, so the self-coer-cive force of logicality is mobilized lest anybody ever start think-ing—which as the freest and purest of all human activities is the very opposite of the compulsory process of deduction."

Too many of Israel's American supporters have stopped thinking, in submission to idolatry of Israel. Ironically, as Israel becomes more and more unpopular, the perceived identification of Jews with Israel could invigorate the now-feeble ideology of anti-Semitism, just as Jews' perceived connections to unpopular European rulers fanned the flames of earlier Jew-hatred.

Scott Handleman is studying law at Boalt, at the University of California, Berkeley.

Alexander Cockburn
My Life as an "Anti-Semite"

RIGHT IN THE WAKE OF THEN-HOUSE MAJORITY LEADER Dick Armey's explicit call in mid-2002 for two million Palestinians to be booted out of the West Bank, and East Jerusalem and Gaza as well, came yet one more of those earnest articles accusing a vague entity called "the left" of anti-Semitism. This one was in Salon, by a man called Dennis Fox, identified as an associate professor of legal studies and psychology at the University of Illinois. Salon titled Fox's contribution, "The shame of the pro-Palestinian left: Ignorance and anti-Semitism are undercutting the moral legitimacy of Israel's critics".

Over the past 20 years I've learned there's a quick way of figuring out just how badly Israel is behaving. You see a brisk uptick in the number of articles here accusing the left of anti-Semitism. These articles adopt varying strategies, but the most obvious one is that nowhere in them is there much sign that the author feels it necessary to concede that Israel is a racist state whose obvious and provable intent is to continue to steal Palestinian land, oppress Palestinians, herd them into smaller and smaller enclaves and ultimately drive them into the sea or Lebanon or Jordan or Dearborn or the space in Dallas-Fort Worth airport between the third and fourth runways (the bold Armey plan).

Eschewing these realities, the author feels entirely at liberty to stigmatize the left as stained with anti-Semitism.

The real problem is most Jews here just don't like hearing bad things said about Israel, same way they don't like reading articles about the Jewish lobby here. Mention the lobby and someone will rush into print saying "Cockburn toys with the old anti-Semitic canard that the Jews control the press".

Back in the 1970s when muteness on the topic of how Israel was treating Palestinians was near total in the United States, I'd get the "anti-Semite" slur hurled at me once in a while for writing about such no-no stuff as Begin's fascist roots in Betar, or the torture of Palestinians by Israel's security forces. I minded then, as I mind now, but overuse has drained the term of much clout. The other day I even got accused of anti-Semitism for mentioning that the Jews founded Hollywood, which they most certainly did, as Neil Gabler recently recounted in a very funny, pro-Semitic book.

So cowed are commentators (which is of course the prime objective of those charges of anti-Semitism) that even after the US Congress recently voted full-throated endorsement of Sharon and Israel, with only two senators and 22 US reps voting against, you could scarcely find a mainstream paper prepared to analyze this astounding demonstration of the power of AIPAC and other Jewish organizations lobbying for Israel.

The encouraging fact is that despite the best efforts of the Southern Poverty Law Center to prove that the Nazis are about to march down Main Street, there's remarkably little anti-Semitism in the US, and none that I've ever been able to detect on the American left, which is of course amply stocked with Jews. It's comical to find people like Fox trudging all the way back to the 60s to dig up the necessary anti-Semitic jibe. The less encouraging fact is that there's not nearly enough criticism of Israel's disgusting conduct towards Palestinians.

On a cruise organized by The Nation magazine in late 2002 I was on a panel about nuclear proliferation. (Yes, even afloat off Baja California, the liberal conscience is always on guard duty.) Trying to juice up the panel a bit, I remarked that there was one bit of proliferation that seemed to me indisputably okay, which was when the Soviet Union acquired the know-how to make A and H bombs, thus ending the US monopoly on Armageddon, and in my view making the world a safer place. (My position, very shocking to Jonathan Schell, is that every country should have at least one thermonuclear device, if necessary donated by the World Bank along with the "national" flag.)

Nation and MSNBC mini-pundit Eric Alterman was chairing the session. He immediately shed any pretense of neutrality. Was Cockburn, he snarled at the audience, seeing something commendable in the transfer of atomic secrets to the most evil man the world had ever known?

Which shows just how dumb Alterman is, since at least two-thirds of the audience of Nation seniors, the only subscribers who can afford to pony up for these cruises, were either in the Communist Party or in close sympathy with it. A chill silence greeted Alterman's ill-mannered interruption and then one old boy piped up angrily and said that it was the Red Army that saved the day for the Allies at Stalingrad. Then Jonathan Schell remarked that my position was identical to that of Sakharov.

Alterman ended up looking silly, and so I wasn't too surprised when my friend Christine Ten Barge, one of the Nation guests sitting next to me at dinner, reported Alterman was going around saying I was an anti-Semite. Later Chris sent me an account: "He gave me an example of your anti-Semitism, but I cannot remember how it went exactly. It had something to do with your dissing his hero, Izzy Stone. He claims to be Victor Navasky's golden boy, but I think Victor feels sorry for him for some reason. He certainly feels sorry enough for himself. After that panel, I was standing on the deck taking the air and Eric comes storming out, whining, 'Did you hear that? They don't like me', like he was going to take his toys and go home. I said, like a good social worker, 'Maybe you should work on how you respond to them, try less provocation'. And that was the last real conversation I had with him."

Now, as noted above, being called an anti-Semite these days isn't what it once was. The term has been relentlessly cheapened. As Michael Neumann writes in his brilliant piece in this collection, anti-Semitism is "action or propaganda designed to hurt Jews not because of anything they could avoid doing but because they are what they are".

But nowadays people don't flourish the charge of anti-Semitism because they've heard someone quoting the Protocols or saying that the Jews kill Christian babies. Anti-Semitism has become like a flit gun to squirt at every inconvenient fly on the window pane.

Maybe Alterman began to think of me as an anti-Semite after, years ago, I wrote that he was three-quarters brown-noser and one-quarter cheeky chappie. I came to this conclusion after being invited by the spring-heeled Alterman in his Yale days to talk about the press. Since in those days I was the in-house critic at the Village Voice of the policies of the Begin government, young Eric knew what he was getting, but nonetheless positively fell over himself with pleasantries as he led me towards the seminar.

These days, at the Nation and on MSNBC he patrols the Democratic perimeter, nipping at the heels of any view overstepping the bounds of decorous mainstream conversation. The word 'Nader' brings an angry flush to his cheeks. 'Greens' makes him bilious. The cheeky chappie of yesteryear is getting the sour edge that mini-pundits acquire when they realize that mini-pundits are what they are always doomed to remain. When Sharon's F-16s blew away some kids in Gaza, collateral damage in the effort to kill a Hamas leader, Alterman had this to say on his MSNBC site:

"I don't know if killing the military chief of Hamas, together with his family, is an effective military measure—as surely someone will rise to replace him and it will make a lot more people angry, perhaps even angry enough to become suicide bombers. It may not bring Israel and the Palestinians any closer to peace or mutual security. But I don't have a moral problem with it.

"Hamas is clearly at war with Israel. Hamas feels empowered to strike Israeli civilians inside Israel proper and not just on the war zone of the West Bank. Sheik Salah Shehada could have protected his family by keeping away from them. He didn't and owing to his clear legitimacy as a military target, they are dead too.

"So tough luck, fella."

Which is presumably what those Palestinian suicide bombers say as they press the button on their belt amid a crowd of Jewish kids.

I saw 2002 as a year when the Israel lobby was worrying that the grip of the gag rule might be loosening a trifle. Now, the original gag rule was adopted by the US House of Representatives in 1836, resolving that "all petitions, memorials, resolutions, propositions, or papers, relating in any way, or to any extent whatsoever, to the subject of slavery, shall, without being either printed or referred, be laid on the table, and that no further action whatever shall be had thereon".

The parallel gag rule these days concerns Israel, a collective agreement by our legislators and the larger political community that any discussion of the conduct of any government of Israel, of the relationship of the United States to Israel, of the power of the pro-Israel lobby in the United States, be kept as near to zero as is possible.

In the 1970s and early 1980s when I began writing on these issues, the gag rule was riding high, amid general agreement in respectable circles that Israeli Prime Minister Golda Meir was on the money when she declared flatly that there was no such thing as a Palestinian, and when Joan Peters got an enthusiastic reception for her book *From Time Immemorial,* which advanced the mad thesis that Palestinians in Israel were all relatively recent immigrants from adjacent Arab countries.

Things have improved since then, though not for the Palestinians, who in those days had UN Resolution 242 to comfort them, instead of the mini-Bantustans promised them in George Bush's "road map". Here in the US there's general agreement that there are people who can be fairly called Palestinians, though beyond this concession there's no agreement about anything, and Defense Secretary Donald Rumsfeld publicly opines Israel stole the West Bank fair and square and the Palestinians should quit being sore losers and move on.

By 2002 it was getting harder and harder to foster the impression that General Sharon was a man of peace, imbued with a constructive vision of communal relations in the Holy Land. As the dust rose above demolished homes on the West Bank and the enduring terror of the occupation provoked retaliatory terror in the form of the ghastly, futile suicide bombings, the predictable warnings against anti-Semitism began to appear in the liberal and left press. Then, it's clear, the Israel lobby decided to enforce the gag rule, by working successfully for the ouster of two members of Congress who had defied it.

A torrent of money from out of state American Jewish organizations smashed Earl Hilliard, the first elected black congressperson in Alabama since Reconstruction, and you could have heard a mouse cough. Hilliard had made the fatal error of calling for some measure of even-handedness in the Middle East. So he was targeted by AIPAC and the others. Down he went, defeated in the Democratic primary by Artur Davis, a black lawyer who obediently sang for his supper on the topic of Israel.

Then it was Cynthia McKinney's turn. An excellent liberal black congresswoman, McKinney hadn't been cowed by the Israel-right-or-wrong lobby and had called for a proper debate on the Middle East, and for a real examination of the lead-up to 9/11. The sky duly fell in on her. American Jewish money showered upon her opponent, Denise Majette. Buckets of sewage were poured over McKinney's head in the Washington Post, and Cynthia Tucker, the black editorial in-house pundit at the Atlanta Journal-Constitution, declared McKinney to be "a fringe lunatic, well outside the congressional mainstream".

Tucker asserted McKinney is "incapable of aiding any cause" and had the final pious effrontery to declare: "The plight of the Palestinians and their desire for an independent homeland is a serious cause deserving of thoughtful, mainstream advocates. Hilliard wasn't one and neither is McKinney."

McKinney's opponent in the primary, Denise Majette, was a former judge best known for her ardent support of Alan Keyes, a black aspirant for the Republican nomination whose prime plank was opposition to abortion. Normally a foe of choice would have brought the women's movement racing to the rescue. Not in McKinney's case.

McKinney saw what happened to Hilliard, and that American Jewish money was pumping up Majette's challenge. So she went to Arab-American groups to try to raise money to fight back. This allowed Tom Edsall to attack her in the Washington Post as being in receipt of money from pro-terror Muslims. Lots of nasty looking Arab/Muslim names suddenly filled Edsall's stories.

Down went McKinney.

We still await Ms. Tucker's thoughtful proposals for a Palestinian homeland, or even a "serious" consideration of the Palestinians' plight.

Oh, and when furious blacks start denouncing the role of outside Jewish money in the onslaughts on Hilliard and McKinney, what then? First stage: imply the money from Jewish-American groups came in reaction to money from Arab-American groups, as with this typical AP paragraph: "Middle East politics played an unlikely role in the race. McKinney drew campaign financing from out of state, including money from pro-Arab groups, while Jewish groups helped fund Majette's campaign. The race echoed the Alabama primary this year that cost Democratic Rep. Earl Hilliard his job. Hilliard received support from Arab groups after supporting a Palestinian state, while his young opponent had the backing of pro-Israel groups."

Then it was Rep. James Moran's turn, in hot water over his head for having remarked in a March 3 town hall session with his constituents that, as quoted in the Virginia-area newspapers, "if it were not for the strong support of the Jewish community for this war with Iraq, we would not be doing this".

The House and Senate Democratic leaders, Nancy Pelosi and Tom Daschle, hastened to denounce Moran's remarks, and six Jewish House Democrats took it upon themselves to advise Moran that he not seek re-election in 2004. Should he do so, "we cannot and will not support his candidacy". Moran was forced to give up on his positions as Democratic Party leader in the mid-Atlantic region. The game plan is clearly what it was with Hilliard of Alabama and McKinney of Georgia: breathe a word about justice for Palestinians, and you'll lose your seat. Moran said he'll certainly run again, and the decision will belong to the voters of his district.

One reason Moran got attacked so hysterically is that Jewish nerves were raw on precisely the point he raised, the role of Jewish opinion here in pressing for the attack on Iraq. It was one thing for Pat Buchanan to raise the issue of dual loyalty in the American Conservative, but when Tim Russert started to press Richard Perle to assure the American people, or at least the audience of "Meet the Press" (by no means the same), that he was advocating an attack on Iraq in the interests of the United States, not some other power, we knew the gag rule had most definitely slackened, if only for a moment.

Suddenly researchers from "Nightline" (one called me on the matter) and other mainstream outfits rushed for copies of "A Clean Break: A New Strategy for Securing the Realm", the 1996 briefing plan for Benjamin Netanyahu prepared by such pro-Israel hawks as Perle, Douglas Feith and others high in the Bush

Administration, advocating attack on Iraq. It was now okay for reporters (Robert Kaiser in the Washington Post, for example) to describe the Jewish neocon lobby for war, starting with Perle, Wolfowitz and Feith, and heading on down the list to Elliott Abrams, running the Israel-Palestine portfolio at the National Security Council.

The op-ed pages duly began to vibrate with predictable charges from people like Lawrence Kaplan of The New Republic that all this talk of dual loyalty and Israel's agenda was nothing but rank anti-Semitism. To his credit, Michael Kinsley, editor of Slate, ran a piece saying that uproar raised by American Jews was probably evidence that Moran was on the money, and that when it came to testimonies to the power of the Jewish lobby, none was more publicly boastful on the matter than AIPAC.

Moran himself was plummeting, whirling in the familiar downward spiral of contrition and self-abasement. But did his remark about "strong support" for attack on Iraq in the Jewish community have any basis in reality? What about American Jewish organizations? In the fall of 2002 the Forward reported that some Jewish groups, such as the Workmen's Circle, were angry at the way the Conference of Presidents of Major American Jewish Organizations had been hijacked by the pro-war faction and by its mad-dog president, Mort Zuckerman, who was openly howling for war in his own publication, U.S. News & World Report, as "the only appropriate and acceptable course".

In mid-September 2002, Michelle Goldberg began a piece on this topic in Salon with "Once a pillar of the American peace movement, mainstream Jewish groups and leaders are now among the strongest supporters of an American invasion of Baghdad." On October 11 the Forward reported that a draft resolution of the 52-member Conference supported "measures necessary to ensure Iraqi disarmament". Jack Rosen, president of the American Jewish Congress, was quoted by the Forward as saying "the final statement ought to be crystal clear in backing the President having to take unilateral action if necessary against Iraq to eliminate weapons of mass destruction".

Abe Foxman of the ADL called the resolution "a consensus document", and the Forward cited him as saying he would support a position that backs the President in "whatever he decides he needs to do".

Of course there were Jewish groups, not least in the big peace coalitions, that were strongly and effectively antiwar. In January the American Jewish Committee released a poll claiming that a majority of American Jews—59 percent—approved of US military action against Iraq to remove Saddam Hussein from power. Thirty-six percent opposed such action. These findings, the AJC also emphasized, were comparable to the attitudes of the general American population. It's at the elite level that the Jewish voices one heard were overwhelmingly pressing for war.

Back once more to Moran. What was the precise nature of his supposedly "anti-Israel" record that the rabbis in his district were now seeking to avenge? In a speech to the American Muslim Council, Moran, who has traveled extensively in the Middle East, said Israeli Prime Minister Ariel Sharon was coming to Washington "probably seeking a warrant from President Bush to kill at will with weapons we have paid for". True enough. In a 1996 Jerusalem Post op-ed, Moran described an Israeli border policeman beating an unarmed Palestinian. "The unarmed youth was held on the ground while police officers armed with guns and clubs climbed over each other's backs to land their own blows on his body", Moran wrote. "Most of the witnesses to this scene said it happens all the time. When Israeli police and Palestinians are concerned there is no justice or fair play. Might makes right. I witnessed the police laughing and making self-congratulatory gestures after the beating."

How encouraging to know that an elected US representative had the sinew to describe such a scene, sinew lacking in most US reporters deployed in Israel. But, alas, such indignation, in Nancy Pelosi's words about Moran's remarks in Virginia, has "no place in the Democratic Party"—or, given the broader Christian evangelical alliance with Sharon, in the Republican Party either.

The spring of 2002 was also when we could enjoy the piquant contrast in the press coverage across the decades of Billy Graham's various private dealings with Nixon, as displayed on the tapes gradually released from the National Archive or disclosed from Nixon's papers. I'll come shortly to the recent flap over Graham and Nixon's closet palaverings about the Jews, but first let's visit another interaction between the great evangelist and his commander in chief. Back in April 1989 a Graham memo to Nixon was made public. It took the form of a secret letter, dated April 15, 1969, drafted after Graham met in Bangkok with missionaries from Vietnam. These men of God said that if the peace talks in Paris were to fail, Nixon should step up the war and bomb the dikes. Such an act, Graham wrote excitedly, "could overnight destroy the economy of North Vietnam".

Graham gave his imprimatur to this recommendation. Thus the preacher was advocating a policy to the US commander in chief that on Nixon's own estimate would have killed a million people. The German high commissioner in occupied Holland, Seyss-Inquart, was sentenced to death at Nuremberg for breaching dikes in Holland in World War II. (His execution did not deter the USAF from destroying the Toksan dam in North Korea, in 1953, thus deliberately wrecking the system that irrigated 75 percent of North Korea's rice farms.) This disclosure of Graham as an aspiring war criminal did not excite any commotion when it became public in 1989, twenty years after it was written. I recall finding a small story in the Syracuse Herald-Journal. No one thought to chide Graham or even question him on the matter.

Very different was the reception of a new tape revealing Graham, Nixon and Haldeman palavering about Jewish domination of the media, with Graham invoking the "stranglehold" exerted by the Jews. On the account of James Warren in the Chicago Tribune, who has filed excellent stories down the years on Nixon's tapes, in this 1972 Oval Office session between the three men, the President raises a topic about which "we can't talk ... publicly", namely Jewish influence in Hollywood and the media.

Nixon cites Paul Keyes, a political conservative who is executive producer of the NBC hit, "Rowan and Martin's Laugh-In", as telling him that "11 of the 12 writers are Jewish". "That right?" says Graham, prompting Nixon to claim that Life magazine, Newsweek, The New York Times, the Los Angeles Times and others are "totally dominated by the Jews". Nixon says network TV anchors Howard K. Smith, David Brinkley and Walter Cronkite are "front men who may not be of that persuasion", but that their writers are "95 percent Jewish". "This stranglehold has got to be broken or the country's going down the drain", the nation's best-known preacher declares.

"You believe that?" Nixon says. "Yes, sir", Graham says. "Oh, boy", replies Nixon. "So do I. I can't ever say that but I believe it." "No, but if you get elected a second time, then we might be able to do something", Graham replies. Magnanimously Nixon concedes that this does not mean "that all the Jews are bad" but that most are left-wing radicals who want "peace at any price except where support for Israel is concerned. The best Jews are actually the Israeli Jews." "That's right", agrees Graham, who later concurs with a Nixon assertion that a "powerful bloc" of Jews confronts Nixon in the media. "And they're the ones putting out the pornographic stuff", Graham adds.

Later Graham says "A lot of the Jews are great friends of mine. They swarm around me and are friendly to me. Because they know I am friendly to Israel and so forth. They don't know how I really feel about what they're doing to this country." After

Graham's departure Nixon says to Haldeman, "You know it was good we got this point about the Jews across." "It's a shocking point", Haldeman replies, "Well", says Nixon, "it's also, the Jews are irreligious, atheistic, immoral bunch of bastards."

Within days of these exchanges becoming public the 83-year-old Graham was hauled from his semi-dotage, and impelled to express public contrition. "Experts" on Graham were duly cited as expressing their "shock" at Graham's White House table talk. Why the shock? Don't they know that this sort of stuff was consonant at that time with the conversational bill of fare at country clubs in America, not to mention many a Baptist soiree. Nixon thought American Jews were pinko peaceniks who dominated the Democratic Party and were behind the attacks on him. Graham reckoned it was Hollywood Jews who had sunk the nation in porn. Haldeman agreed with both of them. At whatever level of fantasy they were all acknowledging power. But they didn't say they wanted to kill a million Jews. That's what Graham said about the Vietnamese and no one raised a bleat. No one hauled him from an earlier stage of dotage to force him to apologize for advocating something pretty close to genocide.

It's supposedly the third rail in political and cultural life here even to have a discussion of Zionist influence in the media. Obviously, Jews don't "control" the media. All the same, Jewish families are proprietors of some of the most powerful newspapers in the country. Is it likely that this has no bearing on their coverage of the Middle East? So, it's reasonable to point out that Jewish families control the New York Times and Washington Post and to put up for discussion whether this affects the editorial stance of both newspapers. But it is also true that the most rabid of all papers in its Israel-right-or-wrong stance is the Wall Street Journal, which is not Jewish owned and whose most influential editor was Robert Bartley, a mid-western Christian.

The economic and political commentator (and former denizen of The Wall Street Journal editorial page) Jude Wanniski remarked in his web newsletter at the time of the Graham uproar that even if Jews don't control the media overall, it is certainly true to say that they control discussion of Israel in the media here.

Some time in the spring of 2002 I wrote an item for a column I was doing at the time for New York Press. Later, the column went up on our CounterPunch website (counterpunch.org), which has around 50,000 regular visitors a day.

"There are a number of stories sloshing around the news now", I wrote, "that have raised discussion of Israel and of the posture of American Jews to an acrid level. The purveyor of anthrax may have been a former government scientist of Jewish ethnic extraction with a record of baiting a colleague of Arab origins, acting with the intent to blame the anthrax on Muslim terrorists.

"Rocketing around the web and spilling into the press are many stories about Israeli spies in America at the time of 9/11. On various accounts of unknown reliability, they were trailing Atta and his associates, knew what was going to happen but did nothing or were simply spying on US facilities. Some posing as art students have been expelled, according to the AP. Finally, there's Sharon's bloody repression of the Palestinians, and Israel's apparently powerful role in Bush's foreign policy."

You'd have thought I'd urged America's youth to immerse themselves in the *Protocols of the Elders of Zion*. People wrote in demanding that I acknowledge the Israeli spy ring story had been "discredited". I declined to do so, citing some very good columns by Justin Raimondo on the antiwar.com site, also the work of reporter John Sugg of the Atlanta-based Creative Loafing alternative weekly chain, and Jane's Intelligence Digest. I could also have mentioned Carl Cameron's four-part series on Fox News, altogether the single most comprehensive overview of Israel's secret war, and Le Monde, as well as Insight, the magazine supplement of the Washington Times.

Jane's put it well, remarking in a March 15 dispatch: "It is rather strange that the US media, with one notable exception, seems to be ignoring what may well prove to be the most explosive story since the September 11 attacks—the alleged break-up of a major Israeli espionage operation in the United States which aimed to infiltrate both the Justice and Defence departments and which may also have been tracking Al-Qaeda terrorists before the aircraft hijackings took place."

At the time I was driving a 1985 Ford Escort (diesel wagon) across the country from South Carolina. As I headed off down the road from Greenville, SC, towards Birmingham, AL, my cellphone rang. It was a fellow from The New Republic called Frank something or other, who said he wanted to quiz me about some recent remarks of mine about the Internet being awash with anti-Israel material. Amid the crackle and hiss of the ether and the roar of the interstate it was hard to hear Frank through the no-hands speaker on my dashboard, but eventually I caught his purpose and asked him flatly, in more-or-less these words, "Frank, is your purpose to accuse me of disseminating anti-Semitic libels, under the guise of relaying rumors on the Internet?" Frank allowed jovially as how that was indeed his intent.

I told him that in my opinion the stories about Israeli spies, as categorized in a US inter-agency report, as discussed on Fox News, by the French site Intelligence Online and various other news sources including the British Jane's, were legitimate topics of comment, as were the stories about anthrax dissemination involving an anti-Arab researcher.

We went back and forth on such issues until the static got too bad. Later I retrieved a magnanimous message from Frank Foer, as his name turned out to be, saying that he was conferring with associates about whether to deal with me in The New Republic.

So I assumed that at some point Cockburn would be stigmatized yet again as the purveyor of anti-Semitic filth.

Eventually Foer's piece, for the online New Republic, tumbled into my inbox, where I read it after enjoying some spectacular barbecue at Dreamland in Birmingham, AL. After a pro forma linking of my name with that of Louis Farrakhan, Foer conceded that I had in the past denounced expressions of anti-Semitism but that was now moot given the fact that in an allusion to Gabler's book on Hollywood I had pointed out that Sam Goldwyn, Bill Fox and another mogul had all grown up within 50 miles of each other in Galicia. In Foer's view this was not the mere relaying by me of an interesting fact but a culpable demonstration of anti-Semitism.

Then he got down to business, focussing on the paragraph quoted above, where I'd brought up the Israeli spy story and the anthrax conundrum. "To be fair", he wrote, "Cockburn doesn't exactly endorse these theories…. Indeed, when I reached Cockburn to ask him about these conspiracies, he insisted he was just reporting what was already in circulation. 'I don't think I said they are true. I don't know there's enough exterior evidence to determine whether they are true or not.'"

"But, of course," Foer crowed, "that last sentence is the giveaway. There most certainly is enough exterior evidence to determine whether the stories are true or not. The answer is that they are not. They are wild rumors circulating, if at all, in some of the least credible corners of the Internet. No respectable media outlet has given these stories credence. Merely by stating that these ideas are in circulation, merely by saying it's impossible to judge their veracity, Cockburn confers these ideas with legitimacy." Case proved.

But … "some of the least credible corners of the Internet"? No one from The New Republic likes antiwar.com and Justin Raimondo, and maybe he was throwing in Fox News but surely not Le Monde and Jane's Intelligence Digest.

"Consider, for example," Foer went on, "the story about the mad Jew scientists out to ruin the Muslims. I searched for it on the Lexis-Nexis news database but came up with nothing—not one single mention of the story in a mainstream news outlet." Foer hadn't tried very hard. A quick punch-through on Google brought four rather lengthy and detailed stories in the "mainstream" media on the harassment of Dr. Ayaad Assaad, a former Fort Detrick scientist, who was driven out of his job by people whose hatred of Arabs seemed to verge on the psychotic. The Hartford Courant ran two long stories: one report on how many samples of deadly anthrax and other bio-terror toxins had gone missing from the Army's Fort Detrick facility, and another on the campaign against Dr. Assaad—the connecting tissue being another Fort Detrick scientist, Dr. Philip Zack, who was video-taped going into the lab at night after hours, and who was at the center of the anti-Assaad clique.

According to the Courant, "Assaad said he was working on the Saturday before Easter 1991, just after the Persian Gulf War had ended, when he discovered an eight-page poem in his mailbox. The poem, which became a court exhibit, is 47 stanzas—235 lines in all, many of them lewd, mocking Assaad. The poem also refers to another creation of the scientists who wrote it—a rubber camel outfitted with all manner of sexually explicit appendages. The poem reads: 'In [Assaad's] honor we created this beast; it represents life lower than yeast.' The camel, it notes, each week will be given 'to who did the least'. The poem also doubles as an ode to each of the participants who adorned the camel, who number at least six and referred to themselves as 'the camel club'. Two—Dr. Philip M. Zack and Dr. Marian K. Rippy—voluntarily left Fort Detrick soon after Assaad brought the poem to the attention of supervisors."

Foer also missed the complete account on the anthrax investigation posted on Salon.com, in a story dated January 26, 2002. Not to mention the Philadelphia Inquirer story, dated February

28, 2002. He also blithely ignores major media coverage of the Israeli spy story. Why should he dally with fact when he was hurrying to issue judgement: "Cockburn's column goes way beyond legitimate criticism of Israel. It's akin to the rantings of pitchfork Pat Buchanan, whose anti-Semitism The Nation has condemned. So you would expect the magazine to take a tough stance on the anti-Semitism in its own backyard. But when I asked The Nation's editor, Katrina vanden Heuvel, about Cockburn, she could only lamely distance herself from the piece: 'This didn't appear in The Nation. I don't read CounterPunch.... It's been our experience that we've had differences with our writers. It's a strength of the magazine that it accommodates a range of perspectives.'"

Isn't it great to have an editor whose first instinct is to stand up for a 20-year veteran of The Nation's columns!

"There are some perspectives that shouldn't be accommodated", Foer concluded.

So you should know that these days it's clear evidence of anti-Semitism to have written an item that pisses off someone at The New Republic, with which I have had combative relations for the past 30 years, as would anyone with a decent moral fiber in his body. Could anyone sink lower than Foer? Yes! Eric Alterman, the above-mentioned brown-noser and cheeky chappie, adduced as a proof of my anti-Semitism the fact that I had been rude, more than once, about Irving Howe. Puts me up there with the Cossacks, doesn't it?

Alexander Cockburn is coeditor of CounterPunch. He lives in Northern California.

Lenni Brenner
Anti-Semitism, Old and New

WE LIVE IN A SINGULAR ERA. THE JEWS HAVE SURVIVED thousands of years of oppression of Judaism as a religion and, in modern times, against them as a race. Today American anti-Semitism has retreated into the wings of politics, yet Judaism and Zionism also are in distinct decline. Every poll confirms what one panelist at a recent New York Zionist establishment seminar emphasized: anti-Semitism based on traditional themes—the Jews as economic exploiters and/or competitors, or as a racial danger to gentiles—"is a fire that has burned itself out".

Every US Jewish establishment poll reports that an ever-diminishing minority of elderly answer "yes" to "Are Jews cheats in business?" etc., while Jews have been elected senators in states with tiny Jewish populations. Jews have become America's role model. Middle-class gentiles who want to send their kids to a good private university rate a school by two criteria: the number of Jewish professors and Chinese students it has.

Yet many, left and right, Jew and gentile, fear that history repeats itself: There will be another great depression. Wall Street will ask central casting for another Hitler to protect it and crush the left. The Jews will be slaughtered. They don't know that Mussolini played with anti-Semitism at the start of his Fascist Party but gave it up when he realized that Italians saw Jews as victims of medieval Papal fanaticism. He had Jews in his cabinet and trained the founders of Israel's navy at his maritime academy. When he finally allied himself to Hitler and imitated Germany's anti-Jewish laws, he lost many crucial supporters.

Most American politicians are murderous but sane. They understand that attacks on Jews qua Jews won't ever sell in a country whose first president welcomed the Jews and assured them of their right to be here.

The rabbis and Zionists despair. A 2001 poll found that 49 percent of our Jews had checked out of Judaism. By now, a majority have abandoned it for atheism. Intermarriage is the norm for young Jews. They are welcome by their new in-laws and the society around them. Zionist recruiters must now focus on "Islamic anti-Semitism". Occasionally a synagogue or individual Jews are attacked in Europe or the US by Muslims. This must be denounced in no uncertain terms by the human rights community. But it is only to be expected. Zionists never stop proclaiming that they represent "the Jews". Is it strange that some ignorant Muslims believe them and equate Judaism with Zionism?

I write only days after Hamas and Islamic Jihad declared a three-month military truce in their suicidal resistance terror-war against Zionist domination of their native land. Whether it is extended primarily depends on the Zionists' response to their demand that Israel end its most blatant forms of oppression. But a lesson has been learned. Attack Israelis as such and you only isolate yourself. If Israel continues to oppress the Palestinians, and Hamas & Co. return to kamikaze resistance, they will lose support among Palestinians and worldwide.

Everyone with a speck of political savvy now understands that the only way to expose and defeat Zionism in the future is to show the world the oppression of Palestinians, and mobilize Palestinians, progressive Israelis and Jews, and the world at large, in demonstrations against those injustices. Progressive Americans must continue to challenge Nazi and Kluxer rallies. History is against them in the long run. But history works through us crushing them in the short run. So history is likewise on our side in the struggle against Zionism. Our focus must be to build a democratic secular movement for one democratic secular Palestinian/Israeli state. That and only that will end all Zionist injustices.

If Hamas is so stupid as to again react militarily against Zionist provocations, we must condemn such atrocities and explain to its ranks that the winning strategy is vast peaceful demonstrations that isolate the Zionist establishment in Israel and the world. All observers agree that old-style anti-Semitism is retreating into oblivion. When Zionism is politically defeated and all Palestinians have full equality in all the land between the Jordan and the Mediterranean, "Islamic anti-Semitism" will likewise lose its popular appeal. But not a minute before. Bluntly put: if you want to end today's "anti-Semitism" against Jews, end Zionism's "anti-Semitism" against Palestinians.

Lenni Brenner is author of Zionism in the Age of the Dictators *and, most recently,* 51 Documents: Zionist Collaboration with the Nazis.

Uri Avnery
Manufacturing Anti-Semites

SADDAM HUSSEIN'S FIRST ISRAELI VICTIM WAS A ZIONIST myth on which we were brought up. According to that myth, Israel is a haven for all the Jews in the world. In all the other countries, Jews live in perpetual fear that a cruel persecutor will arise, as happened in Germany. Israel is the safe haven, to which Jews can escape in times of danger. Indeed, this was the purpose of the Founding Fathers when they established the state.

Then Saddam came along and proved the opposite. All over the world, Jews live in safety, and only in one place on the planet are they threatened by annihilation: Israel. Here the national parks are prepared for mass-graves, here (pathetic) measures against biological and chemical weapons are prepared. Many people are already planning to escape to the communities in the Diaspora. End of a myth.

Another Zionist myth died even before that. The Diaspora, so we learned in our youth, creates anti-Semitism. Everywhere the Jews are a minority, and a minority inevitably attracts the hatred of the majority. Only when the Jews gather in the Land of their Forefathers and constitute the majority will anti-Semitism disappear throughout the world. Thus spoke Herzl, the founder of modern Zionism.

Nowadays this myth, too, is giving up its blessed soul. The very opposite is happening: the State of Israel is causing the resurrection of anti-Semitism all over the world, threatening Jews everywhere.

The Sharon government is a giant laboratory for growing the anti-Semitism virus. It exports it to the whole world. Anti-Semitic organizations, which for many years vegetated on the margins of society, rejected and despised, are suddenly growing and flowering. Anti-Semitism, which has hidden itself in shame since World War II, is now riding on a great wave of opposition to Sharon's policy of oppression.

Sharon's propaganda agents are pouring oil on the flames. Accusing all critics of his policy of being anti-Semites, they brand large communities with this mark. Many good people, who feel no hatred at all towards the Jews but who detest the persecution of the Palestinians, are now called anti-Semites. Thus the sting is taken out of this word, giving it something approaching respectability.

The practical upshot: not only does Israel not protect the Jews from anti-Semitism but, quite on the contrary, Israel manufactures and exports the anti-Semitism that threatens Jews around the world.

For many years Israel enjoyed the sympathy of most people. It was seen as the state of the Holocaust survivors, a small and courageous country defending itself against the repeated assaults of murderous Arabs. Slowly, this image has been replaced by another: a cruel, brutal and colonizing state, oppressing a small and helpless people. The persecuted has become the persecutor, David has turned into Goliath.

We Israelis, living in a bubble of self-brain-washing, find it hard to imagine how the world sees us. In many countries, television and newspapers publish daily pictures of Palestinian children throwing stones at monstrous tanks, soldiers harassing women at the checkpoints, despairing old men sitting on the ruins of their demolished homes, soldiers taking aim and shooting children. These soldiers do not look like human beings in uniform—"the neighbor's son" as they look to Israelis—but like robots without faces, armed to the teeth, heads hidden by helmets, bullet-proof vests changing their proportions. People who have seen these photos dozens and hundreds of times start to see Israel in this image.

For Jews, this creates a dangerous vicious circle. Sharon's actions create revulsion and opposition throughout the world. These reinforce anti-Semitism. Faced with this danger, Jewish organizations are pushed into defending Israel and giving it unqualified support. This support enables the anti-Semites to attack not only the government of Israel but the local Jews, too. And so on.

In Europe, Jews already feel the pressure. But in the United States, they still feel supremely self-confident. In Europe, Jews have learned over the centuries that it is not wise to be too conspicuous and to display their wealth and influence. But in America, the very opposite is happening: the Jewish establishment is practically straining to prove that it controls the country.

Every few years the Jewish lobby "eliminates" an American politician who does not support the Israeli government unconditionally. This is not done secretly, behind the scenes, but as a public "execution". In 2002 this was done to the black congresswoman Cynthia McKinney, a young, active, intelligent and very sympathetic woman. She dared to criticize the Sharon government, support Palestinians and (worst of all) Israeli and Jewish peace groups. The Jewish establishment found a counter-candidate, a practically unknown black woman, injected huge sums into the campaign and defeated Cynthia.

All this happened in the open, with fanfares, to make a public example—so that every senator and congressperson would know that criticizing Sharon is tantamount to political suicide.

Then this process was repeated in a big way. The pro-Israel lobby—which consists of Jews and extreme right-wing Christian fundamentalists—pushed the American administration to start a war. This, too, openly, in full view of the American public. Dozens of articles in the important newspapers pointed this out as a plain political fact.

What will happen if the whole adventure ultimately ends in failure? If it has unexpected negative results? One can easily imagine a whispering campaign starting: "The Jews have pushed us into this"; "The Jews support Israel more than they support America" and, finally, "The Jews control our country."

Furthermore, Sharon may sooner or later bring about a revolution in the Arab world. This will be a disaster for American interests. American Jews, now completely identified with Israel, will be blamed.

Anyhow, the conspicuousness of the Jews in the United States, especially in the media, and their disproportionate influence over the Congress and the White House, can backfire one of these days.

Of course, the special political culture of the United States encourages such phenomena—but that was also true in Spain of the "Golden Age" and the Weimar republic in Germany. History does not have to repeat itself, but neither should one disregard its lessons.

There are people in Israel, people who secretly wish for the victory of anti-Semitism everywhere. That would confirm another Zionist myth on which we were brought up: that Jews will not be able to live anywhere but in Israel, because anti-Semitism is bound to triumph everywhere. But the United States is not France or Argentina; it plays a critical role in the Middle East. Israel's national security, as established by all Israeli governments since Ben-Gurion, is based on the total support of the United States—military, political and economic.

If I were asked for advice, I would counsel the Jewish communities throughout the world as follows: Break out of the vicious circle. Disarm the anti-Semites. Break the habit of automatic identification with everything our governments do. Let your conscience speak out. Return to the traditional Jewish values of "That which is altogether just shalt thou follow!" (Deuteronomy 16,20) and "Seek peace and pursue it!" (Psalms 34, 14). Identify yourselves with the Other Israel, which is struggling to uphold these values at home.

All over the world, new Jewish groups that follow this way are multiplying. They break yet another myth: the duty of Jews everywhere to subordinate themselves to the edicts of our government.

Yuri Avneri is an Israeli journalist, peace activist and former Knesset member.

Linda Belanger
Words Hurt, But Tanks Kill:
Putting Accusations of Anti-Semitism in Context

CANADA HAS BEEN IN THE MIDST OF YET ANOTHER DEBATE on anti-Semitism. This time, the uproar was spurred by statements made by David Ahenakew, a native leader and recipient of the Order of Canada. Ahenakew's statement that Hitler was right "to fry 6 million of those guys because they were taking over" is disgusting, and his membership in the Order of Canada should be withdrawn immediately. However, I can no longer contain my resentment over the endless superficial and pointless discussions, interviews and opinions on "growing anti-Semitism".

One particular dialogue on CBC radio left me steaming for days. Upon sitting down and analyzing the reason for my anger I concluded that it is not so much what was said as what was not said that disturbed me. The idea put forward by one of the participants posited that since most Jews are Zionists, one cannot claim to be anti-Zionist without being anti-Semitic. Neither the host nor the other two participants in the discussion saw fit to challenge this opinion. This idea must be challenged in the strongest terms each and every time it is put forth. It is not racist to oppose a racist ideology. If it is true that most Jews are Zionists, they must be offered the many sound intellectual arguments that contest this ideology. It is not up to the rest of the country to accept it.

As usual in this type of discussion, one is made to feel that Jews are more victimized than other groups or that anti-Semitism is somehow more abhorrent than other forms of racism. Although reference was made to bomb threats against synagogues and Jewish schools, there was not one reference to threats made to mosques and the current hate literature being published on Muslims and Arabs by the Zionist-dominated media.

Typically, only one participant touched upon what he referred to as "the situation in the Middle East in regards to Palestinians". I suppose this vague statement was intended to raise the issue of a possible link between rising anti-Semitism and the Israeli policies in the West Bank and Gaza: policies that include 24-hour curfews for months, home demolitions, destruction of ancient olive groves, roadblocks that prevent access to education, jobs and healthcare and total disregard for over 65 United Nations resolutions. The rank hypocrisy of talking about offensive words, no matter how stupid, racist and ignorant, in regards to Jews and the Holocaust while ignoring what is actually happening to Palestinians right now must surely be offensive to any intelligent listener.

The Zionists' supporters will argue that Israel is held to higher standards than other nations. But Israel proclaims itself to be a bastion of freedom, democracy and justice. Nations like Israel, Canada, the United States and Britain should be held to higher standards than developing countries with undemocratic governments and large uneducated populations. There can be no discussion regarding growing anti-Semitism without consideration of the Israeli apartheid system imposed on Palestinians. Although I am not of Arab background, my anger at this injustice is intense. Fortunately it is tempered by age and experience. My parents often repeated to me that there are good and bad in every race; time has proved them right. I have also had the good fortune of becoming acquainted with Jews who see the injustices being perpetrated on Palestinians. Since a young age I have turned to writing when I am sad or angry.

What of the children of people of Arab descent? Both Canada and the US have substantial Arab and Muslim populations whose sympathies clearly lie with Palestinians. How is the testosterone-charged teenager of Arab descent going to react to news that 8-year-old children of a group he identifies with are being shot for throwing rocks at tanks or sometimes just shot in the back? What is this kid going to do when he hears lengthy discussions about anti-Semitism on radio and television and nothing about the crimes committed against his own kind? I can bet it will not be to write. Talk of anti-Semitism without looking at the context may be a way to fill air time without generating the ire of B'nai B'rith but in no way contributes to reducing anti-Semitism. Real solutions come as a result of discussion by an informed public. There is no winning through suppression of information and discussion. You can keep the lid on the pressure cooker for only so long before it blows up.

Since my early teens I have heard in reference to the Holocaust, "It must not happen again". This is a wise statement that has become part of our moral fiber. But "It" is happening again—to Palestinians. Sympathy for Jews and revulsion for Hitler and the Holocaust must not be carried beyond the bounds of logic. It must end when the victim becomes the oppressor, otherwise we have learned nothing.

The pro-Israel camp is quick to point out that Arabs are not sufficiently critical of Palestinian suicide attacks on Israelis. But how often does one hear Jews condemning the Israeli policies of aggression on the entire Palestinian population? I blame the media for this as much as Jews, because I know that there are Jews who passionately condemn and actively oppose Israeli apartheid. By giving air time to the whining Zionists with their preposterous precepts and not to the "left-wing" Jews who oppose the policies of the war criminal Ariel Sharon and his ilk, the media is contributing to anti-Semitism and condoning the racist Zionist policies that are completely irreconcilable with our values of freedom and equality.

Linda Belanger lives in Canada.

Bruce Jackson
Jews Like Us

THEY'RE SPREADING POISON ABOUT AMERICAN JEWS. Many of the people spreading this poison are Jews themselves, a relatively small group that wants to convince everybody (or at least everybody in power) that the great bulk of us think the way they do, which we don't. Some non-Jews, like Pat Buchanan and other less-rabid but no less invidious bigots, also find it a good way to stereotype us: Jews all think alike, dontcha know. It's weird and freaky when militant right-wing Jews can hook up with old-fashioned anti-Semites to stereotype the rest of us, but these are weird and freaky times.

The basic tenets of the present poison seem to be these:

- American Jews support Israel's policies whatever they are;
- American Jews believe the settlements in the Occupied Territories are a God-given right;
- American Jews believe Ariel Sharon has peace on his mind but can't get there only because evil Palestinians keep blowing themselves up and forcing him to respond by blowing up or driving tanks through their families' houses and orchards;
- American Jews think all issues of world peace must be subsumed to Israel's security, as defined by the Israeli government;
- American Jews favor current US unilateralism and have contempt for the United Nations because it is full of mean little countries that don't like Israel.

And most important of all: any American Jew who rejects the aforementioned is a "self-hating Jew".

Self-hating Jews

Could any goy have thought that one up? "You disagree with my politics, therefore you are a self-hating Jew. The problem, the ethical issues, the guilt are all yours." Freud would have danced all over it.

You respond, "No, man, you're WRONG about all of it. Let's go over the facts."

They listen, politely, or not, and at the end they say, "See? I told you, you're a self-hating Jew."

True believers of whatever stripe find ratification wherever they look. In the court where the conclusion is foregone, all facts serve only to convict.

I first heard the phrase 'self-hating Jew' in Greenwich Village in the 1980s when a group from the Jewish Defense League, Meyer Kahane's militant organization, stood in the street yelling it at William Kunstler's house. I looked out the window, saw the bared teeth and raised fists and thought that they looked and comported themselves very much like Hitler Jugend, missing only the armbands.

Kunstler's comment on them was, "Pay them no mind. They don't know what they're talking about. That's the silliest thing to call me. I don't hate myself. Everybody knows I love myself."

I went out of the house and before I'd even stepped from the doorway to the top of the steps they were yelling "Self-hating Jew! Self-hating Jew!" at me. I yelled back, "But you don't even know if I'm Jewish." They didn't care. They kept yelling "Self-hating Jew" until I reached the police barricade at Christopher Street, whereupon they started yelling at the house again.

Lunatic Stuff

I'm not making this lunatic stuff up, nor am I waxing rhetorical.

All reliable studies and surveys show that the great majority of American Jews, whatever the level of their support for Israel itself, oppose unilateralism, think the United Nations an important forum, favor a Palestinian state, are opposed to the settlements in the Occupied Territories, oppose Sharon's militancy, are sickened and appalled by the images of Israeli tanks destroying homes, villages and vineyards, and are desperate for the killing and dying on both sides to stop now. Not after every potentially suicidal Palestinian is wiped out. Not after the world is made perfect. Now.

The neocon and radical right, though a numerical minority, have politicians running scared. One example of that is New York Senator Charles Schumer, who recently told students at an upstate Catholic military school that he was now in favor of pre-emptive wars. "Pollster John Zogby said Schumer's tough posture is a political move to appeal to pro-war upstate voters and elements of the Jewish community in New York City", wrote Buffalo News Washington bureau chief Doug Turner. "'I think he's bidding for the Likud vote,' Zogby joked, referring to the party of Israeli Prime Minister Ariel Sharon."

Given the evidence of those surveys, why do Schumer and otherwise sensible members of Congress act as if these bullies of the right represented even a large minority of us? Maybe for the same reason they continue to base US Caribbean policy on the hysterical voices of the small Cuban exile community in Miami. Remember how Al Gore (D), Dan Burton (R) and so many of the rest fell over one another trying to be politically correct and make political capital in the Elian Gonzalez soap opera three years ago? They're terrified of groups of middle-class people who scream at them, and they think such screamers are more likely to vote and write checks than people who speak softly or rationally.

More and more I hear that those militaristic Jews in and advising the Bush administration—such as Paul Wolfowitz inside the White House and William Kristol on the outside—prove where Jews are politically. Nonsense. That only proves what political stripe of Jews are in favor in the Bush White House.

Wolfowitz and Kristol are Americans who are Jewish and who are part of the American conservative right. Why single them out as Jews and then blame the rest of us Jews for them? Most of us don't like or agree with those ideologues either. Blaming the rest of us for them is like blaming the Methodists for Dick Cheney or Baptists for John Ashcroft. It's not the religion that made those people what they are. Wolfowitz, Kristol, Cheney and Ashcroft would be the way they are if they were Zoroastrians.

Jews Like Us

In spring 2001, I started working on a book the working title of which is "Jews like us". I thought it might be useful to give some of the Jews who don't scream a chance to say what they think about being Jewish in America now. I stopped working on the book when everything got cranked up after 9/11, but I've started doing interviews again. I have basically one question I ask everybody: "You say you're Jewish. What do you mean by that?"

The responses are astonishing in their variety. I'm continually amazed at the huge range of stories, opinion and analysis. The only generalization I can make about it is this: hardly any of it comes close to the militant neocon line. Sure, there are some groups in which the ideology is locked down tight and some individuals for whom Sharon's version of Israel's security needs transcends all reason and decency. But that's the minority. Painting us all with the Wolfowitz-Kristol brush, saying, in effect, that our considered political and ethical opinions are worthless, is just today's trendy way to be anti-Semitic, no matter who is doing it.

There is an ever-growing number of organizations of American Jews trying to get the word out that the press and politicians should look beyond the noisy minority. (Just glance at the web sites of Jewish Voices for Peace, Jews for Peace in Palestine and Israel, Not in My Name, Jews Against the Occupation and Brit Tzedik v'Shalom.) Thus far, they seem to have made little impact. Their activities get almost no coverage in the press and few members of Congress consider them the same kind of threat as the militant right or the neocons.

Perhaps they've been too polite. Perhaps they will have to start making the same kind of noise that has so frightened Chuck Schumer and so many other powerful people in Washington. Perhaps they will have to remind those politicians that they also vote and write checks, and that of all the things you can accuse us Jews of there is at least one that is true: we remember.

Bruce Jackson is the SUNY Distinguished Professor and Samuel P. Capen Professor of American Culture at the University of Buffalo. He edits the web magazine BuffaloReports.com

Robert Fisk
Why Does John Malkovich Want to Kill Me?

IT USED TO BE JUST A TRICKLE, A STEADY DRIP-DRIP OF HATE mail that arrived once a week, castigating me for reporting on the killing of innocent Lebanese under Israeli air raids or for suggesting that Arabs—as well as Israelis—wanted peace in the Middle East. It began to change in the late 1990s. Typical was the letter that arrived after I wrote my eyewitness account of the 1996 slaughter by Israeli gunners of 108 refugees sheltering in the UN base in the Lebanese town of Qana.

"I do not like or admire anti-Semites", it began. "Hitler was one of the most famous in recent history." Yet compared with the avalanche of vicious, threatening letters and openly violent statements that we journalists receive today, this was comparatively mild. For the Internet seems to have turned those who do not like to hear the truth about the Middle East into a community of haters, sending venomous letters not only to myself but to any reporter who dares to criticize Israel—or American policy in the Middle East.

There was always, in the past, a limit to this hatred. Letters would be signed with the writer's address. Or if not, they would be so ill-written as to be illegible. Not any more. In 26 years in the Middle East, I have never read so many vile and intimidating messages addressed to me. Many now demand my death. And last week, the Hollywood actor John Malkovich did just that, telling the Cambridge Union that he would like to shoot me.

How, I ask myself, did it come to this? Slowly but surely, the hate has turned to incitement, the incitement into death threats, the walls of propriety and legality gradually pulled down so that a reporter can be abused, his family defamed, his beating at the hands of an angry crowd greeted with laughter and insults in the pages of an American newspaper, his life cheapened and made vulnerable by an actor who—without even saying why—says he wants to kill me.

Much of this disgusting nonsense comes from men and women who say they are defending Israel, although I have to say that I have never in my life received a rude or insulting letter from Israel itself. Israelis sometimes express their criticism of my reporting—and sometimes their praise—but they have never stooped to the filth and obscenities that I now receive.

"Your mother was Eichmann's daughter" was one of the most recent of these. My mother, Peggy, who died after a long battle with Parkinson's three and a half years ago, was in fact an RAF radio repair operator on Spitfires at the height of the Battle of Britain in 1940.

The events of September 11 turned the hate mail white hot. That day, in an airliner high over the Atlantic that had just turned back from its routing to America, I wrote an article for The Independent pointing out that there would be an attempt in the coming days to prevent anyone from asking why the crimes against humanity in New York and Washington had occurred. Dictating my report from the aircraft's satellite phone, I wrote about the history of deceit in the Middle East, the growing Arab anger at the deaths of thousands of Iraqi children under US-supported sanctions, and the continued occupation of Palestinian land in the West Bank and Gaza by America's Israeli ally. I didn't blame Israel. I suggested that Osama bin Laden was responsible.

But the e-mails that poured into The Independent over the next few days bordered on the inflammatory. The attacks on America were caused by "hate itself, of precisely the obsessive and dehumanizing kind that Fisk and Bin Laden have been spreading", said a letter from a Professor Judea Pearl of UCLA. I was, he claimed, "drooling venom" and a professional "hate peddler". Another missive, signed Ellen Popper, announced that I was "in cahoots with the archterrorist" bin Laden. Mark Guon labelled me "a total nut-case". I was "psychotic", according to

Lillie and Barry Weiss. Brandon Heller of San Diego informed me that "you are actually supporting evil itself".

It got worse. On an Irish radio show, a Harvard professor—infuriated by my asking about the motives for the atrocities of September 11—condemned me as a "liar" and a "dangerous man" and announced that "anti-Americanism"—whatever that is—was the same as anti-Semitism. Not only was it wicked to suggest that someone might have had reasons, however deranged, to commit the mass slaughter. It was even more appalling to suggest what those reasons might be. To criticize the United States was to be a Jew-hater, a racist, a Nazi.

And so it went on. In early December, I was almost killed by a crowd of Afghan refugees who were enraged by the recent slaughter of their relatives in American B-52 air-raids. I wrote an account of my beating, adding that I could not blame my attackers, that if I had suffered their grief, I would have done the same. There was no end to the abuse that came then.

In The Wall Street Journal, Mark Steyn wrote an article under a headline saying that a "multiculturalist"—me—had "got his due". Cards arrived bearing the names of London "whipping" parlors. The Independent's website received an e-mail suggesting that I was a pedophile. Among several vicious Christmas cards was one bearing the legend of the 12 Days of Christmas and the following note inside: "Robert Fiske [sic]—aka Lord Haw Haw of the Middle East and a leading anti-semite & proto-fascist Islamophile propagandist. Here's hoping 2002 finds you deep in Gehenna [Hell], Osama bin Laden on your right, Mullah Omar on your left. Yours, Ishmael Zetin."

Since Ariel Sharon's offensive in the West Bank, provoked by the Palestinians' wicked suicide bombing, a new theme has emerged. Reporters who criticize Israel are to blame for inciting anti-Semites to burn synagogues. Thus it is not Israel's brutality and occupation that provokes the sick and cruel people who attack Jewish institutions, synagogues and cemeteries. We journalists are to blame.

Almost anyone who criticizes US or Israeli policy in the Middle East is now in this free-fire zone. My own colleague in Jerusalem, Phil Reeves, is one of them. So are two of the BBC's reporters in Israel, along with Suzanne Goldenberg of The Guardian. And take Jennifer Loewenstein, a human rights worker in Gaza—who is herself Jewish and who wrote a condemnation of those who claim that Palestinians are deliberately sacrificing their children. She swiftly received the following e-mail: "BITCH. I can smell you from afar. You are a bitch and you have Arab blood in you. Your mother is a fucking Arab. At least, for God's sake, change your fucking name. Ben Aviram."

Does this kind of filth have an effect on others? I fear it does. Only days after Malkovich announced that he wanted to shoot me, a website claimed that the actor's words were "a brazen attempt at queue-jumping". The site contained an animation of my own face being violently punched by a fist and a caption that said: "I understand why they're beating the shit out of me."

Thus a disgusting remark by an actor in the Cambridge Union led to a website suggesting that others were even more eager to kill me. Malkovich was not questioned by the police. He might, I suppose, be refused any further visas to Britain until he explains or apologizes for his vile remarks. But the damage has been done. As journalists, our lives are now forfeit to the Internet haters. If we want a quiet life, we will just have to toe the line, stop criticizing Israel or America. Or just stop writing altogether.

© The Independent, May 16, 2002

Robert Fisk reports on the Middle East for the London Independent. He is the author of Pity The Nation: The Abduction of Lebanon.

Kurt Nimmo
Poetry as Treason?

I T SEEMS YOU NOT ONLY HAVE TO BE CAREFUL WHAT YOU SAY, as then-White House spokesman Ari Fleischer warned last year, but also what you write, especially if you are an African-American poet with a Muslim name and Marxist politics.

On September 19, 2002, Amiri Baraka, an influential Beat poet and founder of the Black Arts Repertory Theatre in Harlem, read a recent poem, "Somebody Blew Up America" at the Geraldine R. Dodge Poetry Festival at Waterloo Village in Stanhope, New Jersey. Note the following lines from the poem:

> *Who knew the World Trade Center was gonna get bombed*
> *Who told 4000 Israeli workers at the Twin Towers*
> *To stay home that day*
> *Why did Sharon stay away?*

Since Baraka read his poem in September, popular news commentators and powerful political organizations have called for the revocation of his status as poet laureate of New Jersey, an honorary title which pays him a modest salary of $10,000 per year. Even though he wrote the poem in October 2001, ten months before taking on the title as poet laureate, New Jersey Governor James E. McGreevey wants Baraka to resign and apologize.

Obviously, McGreevey doesn't know Baraka too well. "Amiri Baraka ain't never been your Polite Negro Poet", writes Lee Bailey on EUR, a website covering black entertainment and culture. "So you have to wonder what the New Jersey powers-that-be were thinking when they named him Poet Laureate of NJ?" In fact, Baraka warned the governor something like this might happen. "I said, 'Governor, you're going to catch a lot of hell for this,'" Baraka told The New York Times. "He said, 'I don't care.' I said, 'If you don't care, I don't care.'"

But the Anti-Defamation League does care and is leaning on McGreevey to get rid of Amiri Baraka. It's not so easy, however. Baraka was selected by a committee of poets, and New Jersey state law gives the group sole power of selection. They can't oust Baraka, nor can the governor. Baraka will remain poet laureate until July 2004—that is unless the state of New Jersey can find a way to strip him of the title.

Regardless, Shai Goldstein of the ADL said his organization will put the pressure on the state's humanities and arts officials. The ideas expressed in Baraka's poem, according to William Davidson, ADL chairman-elect, are "directly linked with the anti-American xenophobia that caused such destruction and the murder of so many Americans". In other words, Baraka is not much better than Osama bin Laden.

The New Jersey Council on the Arts said it "regrets" what Baraka chooses to think and write, and it doesn't see how he can remain poet laureate. Baraka, the council members said in a statement, is a "remarkable poet", but his poem is "deeply hurtful and painful". One has to wonder if the New Jersey Council on the Arts knows anything about poetry or literature in general, which is often "hurtful" and "painful". Of course, when the "hurt" and "pain" issues from powerful groups, such as the Anti-Defamation League, not even poets have an excuse. They must be purged for their unacceptable utterances.

Before "everything changed", the media simply ignored poets, even when they said outrageous things, even things now considered "anti-American". Few people take poets seriously, even in New Jersey, home of famous poets, including Walt Whitman, William Carlos Williams and Allen Ginsberg. Now, instead of ignoring poets, more than a few Americans condemn them, especially if the poets are Muslim and hold views contrary to the US government—and particularly if those "anti-American" views are broadcast via the corporate media, from the disgusting Bill O'Reilly on Fox News to the pages of The New York Times.

As for Baraka's suggestion that both the US and Israeli government had prior knowledge of the September 11 attacks, there is clear, ample and documented evidence they most certainly did. Consider the following:

Newsbytes reports on September 27, 2001, that employees of Odigo, an instant messaging company in Herzliyya, Israel, received messages warning of the attacks two hours before they occurred. Alex Diamandis, vice president of sales and marketing for Odigo, confirmed that workers in Israel received the messages. The story is subsequently carried by CNN and Ha'aretz in Israel.

On August 11, 2001, US Navy Lt. Delmart "Mike" Vreeland, held in Toronto on US fraud charges and claiming to be an officer in US naval intelligence, gives Canadian authorities a sealed envelope. On September 14, 2001, Canadian jailers open Vreeland's sealed envelope to find a letter detailing attacks against the WTC and Pentagon. Source: The Toronto Star, October 23, 2001, and Toronto Superior Court Records.

On September 6-7, 2001, 4,744 put options (a speculation that stock prices will go down) are purchased on United Air Lines stock. There are only 396 call options (speculation that the stock will go up) at the same time. Many of the United Air Lines puts are purchased through Deutschebank/AB Brown, a firm managed until 1998 by the current executive director of the CIA, A.B. "Buzzy" Krongard. This is reported in The New York Times and The Wall Street Journal.

In June 2001, German intelligence, the BND, warns the CIA and Israel that Middle Eastern terrorists are "planning to hijack commercial aircraft to use as weapons to attack important symbols of American and Israeli culture." The story is reported by Frankfurter Allgemeine Zeitung, September 14, 2001.

During the summer of 2001, Jordanian intelligence intercepts a communication indicating attacks are planned on the WTC. The message is relayed to Washington. Reported by John K.

Cooley of ABC and published in The International Herald Tribune on May 21, 2002.

Summer 2001, Russian intelligence notifies the CIA that 25 terrorist pilots have been specifically training for missions involving hijacked airliners. Reported by Izvestia.

On July 26, 2001, CBS News reports that John Ashcroft has stopped flying commercial airlines due to a threat assessment.

In August 2001, Russian President Vladimir Putin orders Russian intelligence to warn the US government "in the strongest possible terms" of imminent attacks on airports and government buildings. Source: MSNBC interview with Putin, September 15.

Also in August 2001, Dubya receives classified intelligence briefings at his Crawford, Texas, ranch indicating that Osama bin Laden might be planning to hijack commercial airliners. Reported by CBS News and CNN, May 15, 2001.

August through September 2001, French intelligence services warn the FBI of imminent attacks. These are ignored. Reported by AP, May 21, 2002.

In the week prior to September 11, a caller to a Cayman Islands radio talk show gave several warnings of an imminent attack on the US by bin Laden. Reported by MSNBC on September 16.

On May 31, 2002, FBI Agent Robert Wright holds a press conference at the National Press Club describing his lawsuit against the FBI for deliberately curtailing investigations that might have prevented the 9/11 attacks. He uses words like 'prevented', 'thwarted', 'obstructed', 'threatened', 'intimidated' and 'retaliation' to describe the actions of his superiors in blocking his attempts to shut off money flows to Al Qaeda and other terrorist groups. Source: the C-SPAN website.

(The above information provided by Jeff Chelton of the Law Party.)

None of this, of course, was mentioned in The New York Times article on Baraka, nor did O'Reilly mention it when he questioned Baraka's motives or patriotism (and also called him a "pinhead") on Murdoch's Fox News. The New York Times, ADL, and O'Reilly are simply providing their state-assigned service — to engender public amnesia and divert attention from the truth surrounding 9/11 and the role played by US intelligence and the Dubya administration. Pay no attention to the man behind the curtain.

Finally, the following lines of Amiri Baraka's poem should be considered far more inflammatory and indictable by the "powers-that-be" than any accusations of anti-Semitism put forward by the ADL:

Who make money from war
Who make dough from fear and lies
Who want the world like it is
Who want the world to be ruled by imperialism and national
oppression and terror violence, and hunger and poverty?

Kurt Nimmo is a photographer and writer, living in New Mexico.

Will Youmans
The Divestment Campaign

AT THE END OF OCTOBER 2002, SEVERAL HUNDRED college students from all over the United States met in Michigan to further the growing campaign to divest American universities of financial holdings in companies with ties to Israel. The students gathered because they share recognition of the importance of severing the US-Israeli umbilical cord that feeds Israel's destructive military occupation of Palestine. They argue that Israel's discriminatory legal and political structure vis-à-vis the non-citizen Palestinians of the Occupied Territories is at the very least a variant of apartheid—the rights and security of Jews are given priority, even as Israel refers to the Palestinians as a collective "problem", devoid of rights or the need for security.

Reactions to this nascent movement from American opinion leaders have been nothing short of contemptuous. The president of Harvard, and former Treasury Secretary under Bill Clinton, Larry Summers, decried it as "anti-Semitic in effect, if not in intent." A New York Times columnist, or memo-ist rather, wrote that divestment's advocates were "dishonest" and "hypocrites" because they "single out" Israel. Then the original singling out that inspired the divestment campaign shined its ugly head. Ha'aretz reported that Israeli officials were asking for as much as $10 billion in pure aid from the United States. This "proposal" supposedly "stems from the United States' expected campaign against Iraq coupled with the American desire that Israel not interfere with Washington's plans or use IDF troops against Iraq".

That Israel could issue such an absurd request and reasonably expect satisfaction shows that it already enjoys a special status. Why would it need more money for the less costly course of action? Israel would incur additional costs by intervening or using "IDF troops against Iraq", but Israel does the opposite and charges the United States. If the aid is granted, it will be time to send in the auditors to review this fishy financial transaction.

What bewilders me is that so many critics attack the singling out of Israel by the divestment campaign, but are actively supportive of the singling out of Israel as a special ally and worthy recipient of disproportionately high levels of arms, aid and trade. This is a contradiction, because clearly one's biggest ally and model "light among nations" should be held to an extent of scrutiny commensurate with the favoritism bestowed upon it. Harvard Law professor Alan Dershowitz is one of the most avid purveyors of this contradiction. In a piece he published in the Harvard Crimson (9/23/2002), he charges divestment supporters with singling out Israel, then goes on to start three paragraphs with sentences that begin, "Israel is the only", to demonstrate its benevolence.

Clearly, the issue is not "singling out", but criticism, and Israel's supporters have proven again to be intolerant of it. The interesting thing is that the end goal of stopping US aid to Israel is not really anti-Israel; this effort merely seeks American neutrality. Divestment seeks to transform the United States from being overtly pro-Israel to being impartial. No one is saying redirect US aid to the PA or invest all that money in Palestine!

A fantastic aspect to this "singling out" criticism of the divestment movement is the principle it establishes: no activist effort should focus on one area or issue unless it addresses every other one of equal or greater detriment. Only big-shot columnists and prestigious university administrators could have such an idiotically unworkable conception of activism.

Thomas Friedman's suggestion that divestment activists should target Syria first is also laughable. According to him, divestment activists should target a country that American companies do not invest in, which is like boycotting a business that went bankrupt.

His other counter-examples, Egypt and Saudi Arabia, admittedly make more sense. Their human rights records are deplorable and they receive American aid and investment. Israel is still more justified to target since it has a rights-based democratic structure in place for one portion of those living under its jurisdiction. Divestment activists simply demand that Israel extend that structure to everyone under its jurisdiction. No such rights-based structure exists in Egypt, which gets its aid for making peace with Israel, or Saudi Arabia, which functions as the institutionalized guardian of western oil corporations.

Democratizing these will be easier once Israel goes from being what Israeli professor Oren Yiftachel calls an "ethnocracy" to a sincere democracy. The Arab regimes will no longer be able to use Israel's treatment of the Palestinians to divert its people from their own repression and keep the perpetual police state that the threat of Israel is used to justify. After all, these countries will argue that American calls for democracy are hypocritical so long as our biggest ally gets away with apartheid.

There is another important consideration. Israel is much more dependent on trade with American corporations than most other countries are. It is also much more reliant on US foreign aid, of which Israel receives the largest share. Therefore, its social responsibility obligation to US taxpayers, investors and consumers is the highest.

Nobel Peace Prize winner Desmond Tutu and Ian Urbina explained it perfectly: "Divestment from apartheid South Africa was certainly no less justified because there was repression elsewhere on the African continent." Should we really lower our standards for Israel because there are other countries with poor records?

There is a purely pragmatic reason why American patriots should support divestment. Uncritical support of Israel damages America's international stature. Nearly every decent position the United States takes on human rights, refugees, militarism, nuclear proliferation and minority rights is easily deemed an agenda-driven farce due to its contradictory support for Israel. For example, the international community instantly recognized the emptiness of President Bush's citation of UN resolution violations by Iraq as a justification for war. Israel continues to flaunt far more resolutions.

This is not just about ending Israel's apartheidesque oppression of the Palestinians, it is about importing respectability and consistency into American foreign policy. To do that, we must change it where it is needed the most. The United States will never be an honest broker for peace between Israel and the Palestinians so long as its public and private sectors have so much invested in Israel. Israel must be isolated to be vulnerable to international pressure. George W. Bush is not interested in peace beyond its expedience for other policy priorities. American support for Israel shields it from international criticism.

Divestment is not a knee-jerk, anti-Israel reaction as critics maintain. The goal for divestment is an objective, nonpartisan American policy to replace its destructive pro-Israeli bias, which ultimately furthers the wasting of lives on both sides. Divestment advocates seek to disconnect Israel from America's womb. This does what the United States has failed to do: treat Israel as another country in the world's community of nations. It is time Israel face the responsibilities and expectations codified in international law and necessary for a peaceful resolution to its conflict with the land's natives.

Divestment is fundamentally a strategy for peace. It is a healthy, morally-sound and practical singling out of Israel.

Will Youmans has been studying law at Boalt, at the University of California, Berkeley. He is a member of Students for Justice in Palestine.

M. Shahid Alam
A New Theology of Power

"**T**HIS BOOK SOUNDS AN ALARM: ISRAEL, THROUGH the deep and pervasive power of its lobby, threatens deeply-cherished American values—especially free speech, academic freedom and our commitment to human rights."

That was Paul Findlay, *They Dare To Speak Out* (1985).

In 1982, Paul Findley went down in his re-election bid after serving in the Congress for twenty-two years. The principal pro-Israeli lobby in Washington took credit for his defeat. What was the Congressman's crime? He had crossed a line drawn by the Israeli lobby in the United States; he had violated the ban on meeting Arafat.

Not so long ago I too had a small taste of the same medicine. No, I am not a public figure, nor had I met with Arafat or any other Palestinian degraded to "terrorist" ranks by Israel's lexical offensive. I am only a professor, an obscure peddler of dissent, who, once tenure was secured, had been left reasonably well alone by school administrators, colleagues and assorted self-appointed censors. How then did I get into trouble?

I began to cross that thin line that I should have known one crosses only at some peril. I began to talk and write about Israel. None of this would have been newsworthy if I had been reading from the script; but I was not. Instead, I began calling a spade a spade. In other words, I was stepping over the line. Although invisible, this line is like a charged electrical cable.

I first stepped on this cable when I spoke at a seminar about September 11 at Northeastern University in October 2001. I had planned on providing a historical backdrop to the attacks on the Twin Towers, drawing attention to the record of French, British and American interventions in the region. My principal concern was that such an attempt, so soon after September 11, might be greeted with hostility.

To my pleasant surprise, I was proved wrong. At the end of the seminar, not a few stepped forward to thank me for speaking out. But the matter did not end there. I was informed by the Chair of my department soon after the talk that a colleague had e-mailed to complain that I had departed from the announced theme of the seminar. Later, the same day, as I was walking across the campus, I was stopped by a professor who informed me that he was at my talk, and he proceeded to accuse me of "hate speech". Apparently, he had been troubled by a passing reference to the peculiar history of Israel.

The impact of September 11 on the lives of Americans was best summed up by the feeling that it had changed everything. I shared in America's grief at the wanton loss of human lives, the first in their recent history; though I had known this grief before, many times before. September 11 was changing me too. I was witnessing the curtailment of civil liberties in the United States, growing attacks on Islam, and the triumph of lobbies who wanted the United States to wage endless wars against the rest of the world. I decided to step out of my academic shell. It was time to speak to some real issues.

Among other things, when a campaign for the academic boycott of Israel was initiated in early April 2002, I decided to join the campaign. When I invited a few colleagues to join the boycott, one described the boycott as destructive, prompting me to explain why I thought this campaign was morally justified. I did so in an essay, "An Academic Boycott of Israel", which was first published on www.counterpunch.org on July 31. Of course, this prompted both angry and supportive e-mails; only one threatened violence. On the whole I was pleased at the response.

There was worse to come. On September 3, the Jerusalem Post carried a report on my essay, without any mention of its title or substance, under the heading, "US Prof Justifies Palestinian

Terror Attacks". This provoked more angry e-mails to me, the Chair of Economics and some others at Northeastern University. Over the next two days, I was also contacted by The Jewish Advocate, Boston Herald, Bloomberg News and "The O'Reilly Factor". Although flattered by the attention, I declined the invitation to meet Mr. O'Reilly.

On September 5, taking the cue from the Post, the Herald published another malicious and sensational report on my essay. It was headlined, "Prof Shocks Northeastern with Defense of Suicide Bombers". It claimed that my article "sent shockwaves through the Fenway campus", but quoted only one of my colleagues. This report too made no mention of the title or substance of my essay. And although I had responded in a timely manner to his e-mail, the reporter claimed that he could not contact me by phone or e-mail.

It is curious how these reports had inverted the objective of my essay, which made a case for an academic boycott, a quintessentially nonviolent act, as an alternative to the recent Palestinian acts of desperation. By showing greater solicitude for the Palestinians' desperate plight, I argued, international civil society could give hope to this oppressed people, and persuade them to act with greater patience in the face of Israel's brutal military occupation. The Post and Herald had twisted a moral case for nonviolent action into justification for terror.

It would appear that I had crossed the line in advocating an academic boycott of Israel, and I had to be punished. To quote from Taha Abdul-Basser (Herald, September 9, 2002), what the Post and Herald "actually find distasteful is the thought that intelligent, well-spoken people of conscience should call for a moral stand against the oppressive and unjust behavior of Israel". At least in the United States, it is the Israeli narrative that has dominated public discourse on policies towards the Middle East. This narrative speaks only of Jewish claims to Palestine, and presents Israel as a victim of Arab hatred of all things

Western, a beleaguered outpost of Western civilization in an ocean of Arab barbarians. My essay was unacceptable because it questions this narrative.

As I was finishing this essay on the night of September 8, 2002, I learned that I had been 'spoofed'—a new word in my lexicon. Someone had stolen my identity and sent out a malicious e-mail to administrators and colleagues at Northeastern. The spoof was quite crude, making it hard for anyone to believe it could have originated from me.

In the days following the September 11 attacks, President Bush had advanced a vision of the world framed in Manichean terms. You are either with us, or you are against us. We are innately good, but all those who oppose us are evil-doers; their violence against us is metaphysical, it springs from their devilish nature, and has no political or sociological causes. Instantly, this political doctrine was also transformed into a theology. It applied not only to countries but also to individuals, aliens and citizens alike. Any dissent from the Bush doctrine could be regarded as blasphemous, as support for terrorism. This is the new theology of power, whose foundations and ramifications are being worked out feverishly every day by hawks of every stripe.

In the same manner that Israel, Russia, China, India, and many smaller powers besides, have appropriated this new theology to suppress the legitimate resistance of various oppressed peoples as terrorist activities, a variety of hawkish lobbies have been using the media to stifle discourse by painting their opponents with the brush of terrorism. In attacking me, the Post and Herald reports employed the same strategy.

I am afraid that if these efforts are allowed to succeed, we may soon witness the narrowing or, worse, the closing, of all discourse on history, foreign policy, rights, justice, resistance, violence, power, oppression, sanctions, imperialism and—lest I be accused of offering a partial list—terrorism. We will be free only to mouth slogans.

Down with terrorism! Down with our enemies! Down with Islam!

M. Shahid Alam is a professor of economics at Northeastern University, Boston. He is the author of Poverty from The Wealth of Nations.

Norman Finkelstein
Counterfeit Courage: Reflections on "Political Correctness" in Germany

N 2002 I WAS INVITED, FOR THE SECOND TIME IN AS MANY years, to present a book in Germany. A year earlier Piper published *The Holocaust Industry: Reflections on the Exploitation of Jewish Suffering* and in 2002 Hugendubel put out *Image and Reality of the Israel-Palestine Conflict*. In significant respects, the receptions differed: *The Holocaust Industry* generated much public interest; *Image and Reality* relatively little. No doubt the reason is that Germans have a huge stake in the legacy of the Nazi holocaust but rather little in a just resolution of the Israel-Palestine conflict. It would seem that this order of priorities, although understandable, is to be regretted. The Nazi holocaust, however horrific and even if forever a part of Germany's present, is—except for the handful of survivors—fundamentally a historical question. The persecution of the Palestinians is, by contrast, an ongoing horror, and it is, after all, the crimes of the Third Reich that are used to justify this persecution. In the first instance, moral action by Germans is no longer possible; in the second, it plainly is.

Precisely for this reason I actually looked forward to the recent German trip. I made no secret in my trip a year earlier of my conflicted feelings about promoting *The Holocaust Industry* in Germany. Many close friends and comrades counseled against it and—much more important—I was quite certain that both my late parents would have disapproved. Germans, I was told, could not be trusted to honestly debate Jewish misuses of the Nazi genocide (the subject of *The Holocaust Industry*). In addition, the huge media interest in my book prompted questions—in my opinion, legitimate—about whether I myself wasn't becoming a beneficiary of the industry I deplored. Ultimately I decided that, notwithstanding the real moral risks entailed, I should go to Germany, a decision that, in retrospect, I don't regret.

In the case of the new edition of my book on the Israel-Palestine conflict, such reservations seemed less pertinent. The post-war German generation had just redeemed itself by voting into power a coalition with a resolute antiwar platform. If Germans weren't now ready to honestly debate the Israel-Palestine conflict, when would they be? And no real danger lurked that this book would provoke a media circus if for no other reason than that it wasn't an easy read. Nonetheless, I arrived in Germany with high hopes that just as *The Holocaust Industry* somewhat succeeded, I think, at breaking a harmful taboo, so my new book would perhaps break the taboo on German public discussion of Israel's brutal occupation. With Palestinians facing an unprecedented catastrophe in the event of a new Middle East war, the stakes loom particularly large.

To judge by a steady stream of e-mail correspondence and many conversations, it seems that The Holocaust Industry did stimulate a sober—and much-needed—debate among ordinary Germans. (A handful of neo-Nazis exploited the occasion but, as the dean of Nazi holocaust scholars, Raul Hilberg, observed, German democracy is not so fragile that it can't tolerate a few kooks coming out of the woodwork.) It's still too soon to gauge the popular reaction to the *Israel-Palestine* book. What can already be discerned, however, is the persistence among politically correct Germans of a pronounced animus to my work.

The nadir in the relentless campaign of ad hominem vilification after publication of *The Holocaust Industry* was probably the article in a major German newsweekly, Der Spiegel, claiming in all seriousness that each morning after jogging I meditated on the Nazi holocaust in the company of two parrots. Either Germans had suddenly become engrossed by the (imagined) private life of an obscure Jew from Brooklyn, New York, or—what seems likelier—the personalized attack on the messenger was a deliberate tactic to evade confronting the bad news that the Nazi holocaust had become an instrument of political and financial gain.

During this last trip to Germany, a major state television station, ARD, suggested that I was a publicity hound peddling used goods. This same program wanted, however, to stage a confrontation between me and the Israeli exhibitors at the Frankfurt Book Fair, and to have me denounce on camera a famous Israeli author—both of which I refused to do. It would surely have garnered lots of publicity but I found distasteful the idea of a slugfest between Jews for the amusement of Germans. Even among the politically correct crowd some nasty habits apparently die hard. It is widely known in Germany that both my late parents passed through the Nazi holocaust. This family background has also been shamelessly seized on by politically correct Germans to ridicule and dismiss me as unstable.

Such venomous attacks on a Jew and the son of Holocaust survivors are altogether unique in German public life which is otherwise ever so tactful and discreet on all things Holocaust. One can't but wonder what accounts for them. In fact, the Holocaust has proved to be a valuable commodity for politically correct Germans. By "defending" Holocaust memory and Jewish elites against any and all criticism, they get to play-act at moral courage. What price do they actually pay, what sacrifice do they actually make, for this "defense"? Given Germany's prevailing cultural ambience and the overarching power of American Jewry, such courage in fact reaps rich rewards. Pillorying a Jewish dissident costs nothing—and provides a "legitimate" outlet for latent prejudice. It happens that I agree with Daniel Goldhagen's claim in Hitler's Willing Executioners that philo-Semites are typically anti-Semites in "sheep's clothing". The philo-Semite both assumes that Jews are somehow "different" and almost always secretly harbors a mixture of envy of and loathing for this alleged difference. Philo-Semitism thus presup-poses, but also engenders a frustrated version of, its opposite. A public, preferably defenseless, scapegoat is then needed to let all this pent-up ugliness ooze out.

To account for Germany's obsession with the Nazi holocaust, a German friend explained that Germans "like to carry a load". To which I would add: especially if it's light as a feather. No doubt some Germans of the post-war generation genuinely accepted the burden of guilt together with its paralyzing taboos on independent, critical thought. But today German political correctness is all a charade of pretending to accept the burden of being German while actually rejecting it. For, what is the point of these interminable public breast-beatings except to keep reminding the world: "We are not like them."

It can also be safely said that politically correct Germans know full well that, more often than not, the criticism leveled against Israeli policy and misuse of the Nazi holocaust is valid. In private conversation (as I've discovered) they freely admit to this. They profess to fear that if Jewish abuses become public knowledge, it will unleash a tidal wave of anti-Semitism. Is there really any likelihood of this happening in Germany today? And isn't vigorous and candid debate the best means to stem an anti-Semitic tide: exposing the abuses of the Jewish establishment as well as the demagogues who exploit these abuses for nefarious ends? What politically correct Germans really fear, I suspect, is the loss of power and privilege attendant on challenging the uncritical support of all things Jewish. Indeed, their public defense of the indefensible not only breeds cynicism in political life but, far from combating anti-Semitism among Germans, actually engenders it. Isn't this duplicity typically credited to a dread of, or a desire to curry favor with, a presumed all-powerful Jewry? One also can't but wonder what thoughts run through the heads of politically correct Germans about Jews when the ones they typically consort with, prostrate themselves before in unctuous penance, and publicly laud are known to be the worst sort of hucksters.

The challenge in Germany today is to defend the memory of the Nazi holocaust and to condemn its abuse by American Jewish elites; to defend Jews from malice and to condemn their overwhelmingly blind support for Israel's brutal occupation. But to do this requires real moral courage—not the operatic kind that politically correct Germans so love.

Norman Finkelstein is the author of The Holocaust Industry *and* Image and Reality in the Israel-Palestine Conflict.

Jeffrey St. Clair
Rockets, Napalm, Torpedoes & Lies:
Israel's Attack on the Liberty, Revisited

IN EARLY JUNE OF 1967, AT THE ONSET OF THE SIX DAY War, the Pentagon sent the USS Liberty from Spain into international waters off the coast of Gaza to monitor the progress of Israel's attack on the Arab states. The Liberty was a lightly armed surveillance ship.

Only hours after the Liberty arrived it was spotted by the Israeli military. The IDF sent out reconnaissance planes to identify the ship. They made eight trips over a period of three hours. The Liberty was flying a large US flag and was easily recognizable as an American vessel.

A few hours later more planes came. These were Israeli Mirage III fighters. As off-duty officers sunbathed on the deck, the fighters opened fire on the defenseless ship with rockets and machine guns.

A few minutes later a second wave of planes streaked overhead, French-built Mystère jets, which not only pelted the ship with gunfire but also with napalm bomblets, coating the deck with the flaming jelly. By now, the Liberty was on fire and dozens were wounded and killed, excluding several of the ship's top officers.

The Liberty's radio team tried to issue a distress call, but discovered the frequencies had been jammed by the Israeli planes with what one communications specialist called "a buzzsaw sound". Finally, an open channel was found and the Liberty got out a message to the USS America, the Sixth Fleet's large aircraft carrier, that it was under attack.

Two F-4s left the carrier to come to the Liberty's aid. Apparently, the jets were armed only with nuclear weapons. When word reached the Pentagon, Defense Secretary Robert

McNamara became irate and ordered the jets to return. "Tell the Sixth Fleet to get those aircraft back immediately", he barked. McNamara's injunction was reiterated in saltier terms by Adm. David L. McDonald, the chief of Naval Operations: "You get those fucking airplanes back on deck, and you get them back down." The planes turned around. And the attack on the Liberty continued.

After the Israeli fighter jets had emptied their arsenal of rockets, three Israeli attack boats approached the Liberty. Two torpedoes were launched at the crippled ship, one tore a 40-foot wide hole in the hull, flooding the lower compartments, and killing more than a dozen American sailors.

As the Liberty listed in the choppy seas, its deck aflame, crew members dropped life rafts into the water and prepared to scuttle the ship. Given the number of wounded, this was going to be a dangerous operation. But it soon proved impossible, as the Israeli attack boats strafed the rafts with machine gun fire. Nobody was going to get out alive that way.

After more than two hours of unremitting assault, the Israelis finally halted their attack. One of the torpedo boats approached the Liberty. An officer asked in English over a bullhorn: "Do you need any help?"

The wounded commander of the Liberty, Lt. William McGonagle, instructed the quartermaster to respond emphatically: "Fuck you."

The Israeli boat turned and left.

A Soviet destroyer responded before the US Navy, even though a US submarine, on a covert mission, was apparently in the area and had monitored the attack. The Soviet ship reached the Liberty six hours before the USS Davis. The captain of the Soviet ship offered his aid, but the Liberty's commanding officer refused.

Finally, 16 hours after the attack two US destroyers reached the Liberty. By that time, 34 US sailors were dead and 174 injured, many seriously. As the wounded were being evacuated, an officer with the Office of Naval Intelligence instructed the men not to talk to the press about their ordeal.

The following morning Israel launched a surprise invasion of Syria, breaching the new cease-fire agreement and seizing control of the Golan Heights.

Within three weeks, the Navy put out a 700-page report, exonerating the Israelis, claiming the attack had been accidental and that the Israelis had pulled back as soon as they realized their mistake. Defense Secretary Robert McNamara suggested the whole affair should be forgotten. "These errors do occur", McNamara concluded.

IN ASSAULT ON THE LIBERTY, A FIRST-HAND ACCOUNT BY James Ennes Jr., McNamara's version of events is proven to be as big a sham as his concurrent lies about Vietnam. Ennes's book created a media storm when it was first published by Random House in 1980, including (predictably) charges that Ennes was a liar and an anti-Semite. Still, the book sold more than 40,000 copies, but was eventually allowed to go out of print. Now Ennes has published an updated version, which incorporates much new evidence that the Israeli attack was deliberate and that the US government went to extraordinary lengths to disguise the truth.

It's a story of Israeli aggression, Pentagon incompetence, official lies and a cover-up that persists to this day. The book gains much of its power from the immediacy of Ennes's first-hand account of the attack and the lies that followed.

Now, 35 years later, Ennes warns that the bloodbath on board the Liberty and its aftermath should serve as a tragic cautionary tale about the continuing ties between the US government and the government of Israel.

The Assault on the Liberty is the kind of book that makes your blood seethe. Ennes skillfully documents the life of the average sailor on one of the more peculiar vessels in the US Navy, with an attention for detail that reminds one of Dana or O'Brien. After all, the year was 1967 and most of the men on the Liberty were certainly glad to be on a non-combat ship in the middle of the Mediterranean, rather than in the Gulf of Tonkin or Mekong Delta.

But this isn't Two Years Before the Mast. In fact, Ennes's tour on the Liberty lasted only a few short weeks. He had scarcely settled into a routine when his new ship was shattered before his eyes.

Ennes joined the Liberty in May of 1967, as an Electronics Material Officer. Serving on a "spook ship", as the Liberty was known to Navy wives, was supposed to be a sure path to career enhancement. The Liberty's normal routine was to ply the African coast, tuning in its eavesdropping equipment on the electronic traffic in the region.

The Liberty had barely reached Africa when it received a flash message from the Joint Chiefs of Staff to sail from the Ivory Coast to the Mediterranean, where it was to re-deploy off the coast of the Sinai to monitor the Israeli attack on Egypt and the allied Arab nations.

As the war intensified, the Liberty sent a request to the fleet headquarters requesting an escort. Request denied, by Adm. William Martin. The Liberty moved alone to a position in international waters about 13 miles from the shore at El Arish, then under furious siege by the IDF.

On June 6, the Joint Chiefs sent Admiral McCain, father of the senator from Arizona, an urgent message instructing him to move the Liberty out of the war zone to a position at least 100 miles off the Gaza Coast. McCain never forwarded the message to the ship.

A little after seven in the morning on June 8, Ennes entered the bridge of the Liberty to take the morning watch. Ennes was told that an hour earlier a "flying boxcar" (later identified as a twin-engine Nord 2501 Noratlas) had flown over the ship at a low level.

Ennes says he noticed that the ship's American flag had become stained with soot and ordered a new flag run up the mast. The morning was clear and calm, with a light breeze.

At 9 am, Ennes spotted another reconnaissance plane, which circled the Liberty. An hour later two Israeli fighter jets buzzed the ship. Over the next four hours, Israeli planes flew over the Liberty five more times.

When the first fighter jet struck, a little before two in the afternoon, Ennes was scanning the skies from the starboard side of the bridge, binoculars in his hands. A rocket hit the ship just below where Ennes was standing, the fragments shredded the men closest to him.

After the explosion, Ennes noticed that he was the only man left standing. But he also had been hit by more than 20 shards of shrapnel and the force of the blast had shattered his left leg. As he crawled into the pilothouse, a second fighter jet streaked above them and unleashed its payload on the hobbled Liberty.

At that point, Ennes says the crew of the Liberty had no idea who was attacking them or why. For a few moments, they suspected it might be the Soviets, after an officer mistakenly identified the fighters as MIG-15s. They knew that the Egyptian air force already had been decimated by the Israelis. The idea that the Israelis might be attacking them didn't occur to them until one of the crew spotted a Star of David on the wing of one of the French-built Mystere jets.

Ennes was finally taken below deck to a makeshift dressing station, with other wounded men. It was hardly a safe harbor. As Ennes worried that his fractured leg might slice through his femoral artery leaving him to bleed to death, the Liberty was pummeled by rockets, machine-gun fire and an Italian-made torpedo packed with 1,000 pounds of explosive.

After the attack ended, Ennes was approached by his friend Pat O'Malley, a junior officer, who had just sent a list of killed and wounded to the Bureau of Naval Personnel. He got an immediate message back. "They said, 'Wounded in what action? Killed in what action?'," O'Malley told Ennes. "They said it wasn't an 'action,' it was an accident. I'd like for them to come out here and see the difference between an action and an accident. Stupid bastards."

The cover-up had begun.

THE PENTAGON LIED TO THE PUBLIC ABOUT THE ATTACK ON the Liberty from the very beginning. In a decision personally approved by the loathsome McNamara, the Pentagon denied to the press that the Liberty was an intelligence ship, referring to it instead as a Technical Research ship, as if it were little more than a military version of Jacques Cousteau's Calypso.

The military press corps on the USS America, where most of the wounded sailors had been taken, were placed under extreme restrictions. All of the stories filed from the carrier were first routed through the Pentagon for security clearance, objectionable material was removed with barely a bleat of protest from the reporters or their publications.

Predictably, Israel's first response was to blame the victim, a tactic that has served them so well in the Palestinian situation. First, the IDF alleged that it had asked the State Department and the Pentagon to identify any US ships in the area and was told that there were none. Then the Israeli government charged that the Liberty failed to fly its flag and didn't respond to calls for it to identify itself. The Israelis contended that they assumed the Liberty was an Egyptian supply ship called El Quseir which, even though it was a rusting transport ship then docked in Alexandria, the IDF claimed was suspected of shelling Israeli troops from the sea. Under these circumstances, the Israelis said they were justified in opening fire on the Liberty. The Israelis said that they halted the attack almost immediately, when they realized their mistake.

"The Liberty contributed decisively toward its identification as an enemy ship", the IDF report concluded. This was entirely false, since the Israelis had identified the Liberty at least six hours prior to the attack on the ship.

Even though the Pentagon knew better, it gave credence to the Israeli account by saying that perhaps the Liberty's flag had lain limp on the flagpole in a windless sea. The Pentagon also suggested that the attack might have lasted less than 20 minutes.

After the initial battery of misinformation, the Pentagon imposed a news blackout on the Liberty disaster until after the completion of a Court of Inquiry investigation.

The inquiry was headed by Rear Adm. Isaac C. Kidd. Kidd didn't have a free hand. He'd been instructed by Vice-Admiral McCain to limit the damage to the Pentagon and to protect the reputation of Israel.

Kidd interviewed the crew on June 14 and 15. The questioning was extremely circumscribed. According to Ennes, the investigators "asked nothing that might be embarrassing to Israel and testimony that tended to embarrass Israel was covered with a 'Top Secret' label, if it was accepted at all".

Ennes notes that even testimony by the Liberty's communications officers about the jamming of the ship's radios was classified as "Top Secret". The reason? It proved that Israel knew it was attacking an American ship. "Here was strong evidence that the attack was planned in advance and that our ship's identity was known to the attackers (for it is practically impossible to jam the radio of a stranger), but this information was hushed up and no conclusions were drawn from it", Ennes writes.

Similarly, the Court of Inquiry deep-sixed testimony and affidavits regarding the flag. Ennes, remember, had ordered a crisp new one deployed early on the morning of the attack. The investigators buried intercepts of conversations between IDF pilots identifying the ship as flying an American flag.

It also refused to accept evidence about the IDF's use of napalm during the attacks and chose not to hear testimony regarding the duration of the attacks and the fact that the US Navy failed to send planes to defend the ship.

"No one came to help us", said Dr. Richard F. Kiepfer, the Liberty's physician. "We were promised help, but no help came. The Russians arrived before our own ships did. We asked for an escort before we ever came to the war zone and we were turned down."

None of this made its way into the 700-page Court of Inquiry report, which was completed within a couple of weeks and sent to Adm. McCain in London for review.

McCain approved the report over the objections of Capt. Merlin Staring, the Navy legal officer assigned to the inquiry, who found the report to be flawed, incomplete and contrary to the evidence.

Staring sent a letter to the Judge Advocate General of the Navy disavowing the report. The JAG seemed to take Staring's objections to heart. He prepared a summary for the Chief of Naval Operations that almost completely ignored the Kidd/McCain report. Instead, it concluded:

"[T]hat the Liberty was easily recognizable as an American naval vessel; that its flag was fully deployed and flying in a moderate breeze; that Israeli planes made at least eight reconnaissance flights at close range; that the ship came under a prolonged attack from Israeli fighter jets and torpedo boats".

This succinct and largely accurate report was stamped "Top Secret" by Navy brass and stayed locked up for many years. But it was seen by many in the Pentagon and some in the Oval Office. There was enough grumbling about the way the Liberty incident had been handled that LBJ summoned that old Washington fixer Clark Clifford to do damage control. It didn't take Clifford long to come up with the official line: the Israelis simply had made a tragic mistake.

It turns out that Adm. Kidd and Capt. Ward Boston, the two investigating officers who prepared the original report for Adm. McCain, both believed that the Israeli attack was intentional and sustained. In other words, the IDF knew that they were striking an American spy ship and they wanted to sink it and kill as many sailors as possible. Why then did the Navy investigators produce a sham report that concluded it was an accident?

Twenty-five years later we've finally found out. In June of 2002, Captain Boston told the Navy Times: "Officers follow orders."

It gets worse. There's plenty of evidence that US intelligence agencies learned on June 7 that Israel intended to attack the Liberty on the following day and that the strike had been personally ordered by Israeli Defense Minister Moshe Dayan.

As the attacks were going on, conversations between Israeli pilots were overheard by US Air Force officers in an EC121 surveillance plane overhead. The spy plane was spotted by Israeli jets, which were given orders to shoot it down. The American plane narrowly avoided the IDF missiles.

Initial reports on the incident prepared by the CIA, Office of Naval Intelligence and the National Security Agency all reached similar conclusions.

A particularly damning report compiled by a CIA informant suggests that Moshe Dayan personally ordered the attack and wanted it to proceed until the Liberty was sunk and all on board killed. A heavily redacted version of the report was released in 1977. It reads in part:

"[The source] said that Dayan personally ordered the attack on the ship and that one of his generals adamantly opposed the action and said, 'This is pure murder.' One of the admirals who was present also disapproved of the action, and it was he who ordered it stopped and not Dayan."

This amazing document generated little attention from the press and Dayan was never publicly questioned about his role in the attack.

The analyses by the intelligence agencies are collected in a 1967 investigation by the Defense Subcommittee on Appropriations. Two and half decades later that report remains classified. Why? A former committee staffer said: "So as not to embarrass Israel."

More proof has recently come to light from the Israeli side. A few years after *Assault on the Liberty* was originally published, Ennes got a call from Evan Toni, an Israeli pilot. Toni told Ennes that he had just read his book and wanted to tell him his story. Toni said that he was the pilot in the first Israeli Mirage fighter to reach the Liberty. He immediately recognized the ship to be a US Navy vessel. He radioed Israeli air command with this information and asked for instructions. Toni said he was ordered to "attack". He refused and flew back to the air base at Ashdod. When he arrived he was summarily arrested for disobeying orders.

How tightly does the Israel lobby control the Hill? For the first time in history, an attack on an American ship was not subjected to a public investigation by Congress. In 1980, Adlai Stevenson and Barry Goldwater planned to open a Senate hearing into the Liberty affair. Then Jimmy Carter intervened by brokering a deal with Menachim Begin, where Israel agreed to pony up $6 million to pay for damages to the ship. A State Department press release announcing the payment said, "The book is now closed on the USS Liberty."

It certainly was the last chapter for Adlai Stevenson. He ran for governor of Illinois the following year, where his less than perfect record on Israel, and his unsettling questions about the Liberty affair, became an issue in the campaign. Big money flowed into the coffers of his Republican opponent, Big Jim Thompson, and Stevenson went down to a narrow defeat.

But the book wasn't closed for the sailors either, of course. After a Newsweek story exposed the gist of what really happened on that day in the Mediterranean, an enraged Admiral McCain placed all the sailors under a gag order. When one sailor told an officer that he was having problems living with the cover-up, he was told: "Forget about it, that's an order."

The Navy went to bizarre lengths to keep the crew of the Liberty from telling what they knew. When gag orders didn't work, it threatened sanctions. Ennes tells of the confinement and interrogation of two Liberty sailors that sounds like something straight from the CIA's MK-Ultra program.

"In an incredible abuse of authority, military officers held two young Liberty sailors against their will in a locked and heavily guarded psychiatric ward of the base hospital", Ennes writes. "For days these men were drugged and questioned about their recollections of the attack by a 'therapist' who admitted to being untrained in either psychiatry or psychology. At one point, they avoided electroshock only by bolting from the room and demanding to see the commanding officer."

Since coming home, the veterans who have tried to tell of their ordeal have been harassed relentlessly. They've been branded as drunks, bigots, liars and frauds. Often, it turns out, these slurs have been leaked by the Pentagon. And, oh yeah, they've also been painted as anti-Semites.

In a recent column, Charley Reese describes just how mean-spirited and petty this campaign became. "When a small town in Wisconsin decided to name its library in honor of the USS Liberty crewmen, a campaign claiming it was anti-Semitic was launched", writes Reese. "And when the town went ahead, the U.S. government ordered no Navy personnel to attend, and sent no messages. This little library was the first, and at the time the only, memorial to the men who died on the Liberty."

SO WHY THEN DID THE ISRAELIS ATTACK THE LIBERTY?

A few days before the Six Day War, Israel's Foreign Minister Abba Eban visited Washington to inform LBJ about the forthcoming invasion. Johnson cautioned Eban that the US could not support such an attack.

It's possible, then, that the IDF assumed that the Liberty was spying on the Israeli war plans. Possible, but not likely. Despite the official denials, as Andrew and Leslie Cockburn demonstrate in *Dangerous Liaison,* at the time of the Six Day War the US and Israel had developed a warm covert relationship. So closely were the two sides working that US intelligence aid certainly helped secure Israel's swift victory. In fact, it's possible that the Liberty had been sent to the region to spy for the IDF.

A somewhat more likely scenario holds that Moshe Dayan wanted to keep the lid on Israel's plan to breach the new ceasefire and invade Syria to seize the Golan.

It has also been suggested that Dayan ordered the attack on the Liberty with the intent of pinning the blame on the Egyptians and thus swinging public and political opinion in the United States solidly behind the Israelis. Of course, for this plan to work, the Liberty had to be destroyed and its crew killed.

There's another factor. The Liberty was positioned just off the coast from the town of El Arish. In fact, Ennes and others had used the town's mosque tower to fix the location of the ship along the otherwise featureless desert shoreline. The IDF had seized El Arish and had used the airport there as a prisoner of war camp. On the very day the Liberty was attacked, the IDF was in the process of executing as many as 1,000 Palestinian and Egyptian POWs, a war crime that they surely wanted to conceal from prying eyes. According to Gabriel Bron, now an Israeli reporter, who witnessed part of the massacre as a soldier: "The Egyptian prisoners of war were ordered to dig pits and then army police shot them to death."

The bigger question is why the US government would participate so enthusiastically in the cover-up of a war crime against its own sailors. Well, the Pentagon has never been slow to hide its own incompetence. And there's plenty of that in the Liberty affair: bungled communications, refusal to provide an escort, situating the defenseless Liberty too close to a raging battle, the inability to intervene in the attack and the inexcusably long time it took to reach the battered ship and its wounded.

That's par for the course. But something else was going on that would only come to light later. Through most of the 1960s, the US Congress had imposed a ban on the sale of arms to both Israel and Jordan. But at the time of the Liberty attack, the Pentagon (and its allies in the White House and on the Hill) was seeking to have this proscription overturned. The top brass certainly knew that any evidence of a deliberate attack on a US Navy ship by the IDF would scuttle their plans. So they hushed it up.

In January 1968, the arms embargo on Israel was lifted and the sale of American weapons began to flow. By 1971, Israel was buying $600 million of American-made weapons a year. Two years later the purchases topped $3 billion. Almost overnight, Israel had become the largest buyer of US-made arms and aircraft.

Perversely, then, the IDF's strike on the Liberty served to weld the US and Israel together, in a kind of political and military embrace. Now, every time the IDF attacks defenseless villages in Gaza and the West Bank with F-16s and Apache helicopters, the Palestinians quite rightly see the bloody assaults as a joint operation, with the Pentagon as a hidden partner.

Thus does the legacy of Liberty live on, one raid after another.

Jeffrey St. Clair is coeditor of CounterPunch. He lives in Oregon.

Jeffrey Blankfort
The Israel Lobby and the Left

I T WAS 1991 AND NOAM CHOMSKY HAD JUST FINISHED A
lecture in Berkeley on the Israeli-Palestinian conflict and was
taking questions from the audience. An Arab-American
asked him to explain his position regarding the influence of
America's Israel lobby.

Chomsky replied that its reputation was generally exaggerated and like other lobbies, it only appears to be powerful when its
position lines up with that of the "elites" who determine policy
in Washington. Earlier in the evening, he had asserted that Israel
received support from the United States as a reward for the services it provides as the US's "cop-on-the-beat" in the Middle East.

Chomsky's response drew a warm round of applause from
members of the audience who were no doubt pleased to have
American Jews absolved of any blame for Israel's oppression of
the Palestinians, then in the fourth year of their first intifada.

What is noteworthy is that Chomsky's explanation for the
financial and political support that the US has provided Israel
over the years is shared by what is generically known as the
Israel lobby, and almost no one else.

Well, not quite "almost no one". Among the exceptions are
the overwhelming majority of both houses of Congress and the
mainstream media and, what is equally noteworthy, virtually the
entire American left, both ideological and idealistic, including
the organizations ostensibly in the forefront of the fight for
Palestinian rights.

That there is a meeting of the minds on this issue between
supporters of Israel and the left may help explain why the
Palestine support movement within the United States has been
an utter failure.

Chomsky's position on the lobby had been established well before that Berkeley evening. In *The Fateful Triangle*, published in 1983, he assigned it little weight:

"The 'special relationship' is often attributed to domestic political pressures, in particular, the effectiveness of the American Jewish community in political life and influencing opinion. While there is some truth to this ... it underestimates the scope of the 'support for Israel,' and ... it overestimates the role of political pressure groups in decision making." (P.13)

A year earlier, Congress had applauded Israel's devastating invasion of Lebanon, and then appropriated millions in additional aid to pay for the shells the Israeli military had expended. How much of this support was due to the legislators' "support for Israel" and how much was due to pressures from the Israel lobby? It was a question that should have been examined by the left at the time, but wasn't. Twenty years later, Chomsky's view is still the "conventional wisdom".

In 2001, in the midst of the second intifada, he went further, arguing that "it is improper—particularly in the United States—to condemn 'Israeli atrocities,'" and that the "'US/Israel-Palestine' conflict" is the more correct term, comparable with placing the proper responsibility for "Russian-backed crimes in Eastern Europe [and] US-backed crimes in Central America". And, to emphasize the point, he wrote, "IDF helicopters are US helicopters with Israeli pilots."

Prof. Stephen Zunes, who might be described as a Chomsky acolyte, would not only relieve Israeli Jews from any responsibility for their actions, he would have us believe they are the victims.

In *Tinderbox*, his widely praised (by Chomsky and others) new book on the Middle East, Zunes faults the Arabs for "blaming Israel, Zionism, or the Jews for their problems". According to Zunes, the Israelis have been forced to assume a role similar to that assigned to members of the Jewish ghettoes of Eastern

Europe who performed services, mainly tax collection, as middlemen between the feudal lords and the serfs in earlier times. In fact, writes Zunes, "US policy today corresponds with this historic anti-Semitism." Anyone comparing the relative power of the Jewish community in centuries past with what we find in the US today will find that statement absurd.

Jewish power has, in fact, been trumpeted by a number of Jewish writers, including one, J.J. Goldberg, editor of the Jewish weekly Forward, who wrote a book by that name in 1996. Any attempt, however, to explore the issue from a critical standpoint inevitably leads to accusations of anti-Semitism, as Bill and Kathy Christison pointed out in their article on the role of rightwing Jewish neo-cons in orchestrating US Middle East policy, in CounterPunch (1/25/03):

"Anyone who has the temerity to suggest any Israeli instigation of, or even involvement in, Bush administration war planning is inevitably labeled somewhere along the way as an anti-Semite. Just whisper the word 'domination' anywhere in the vicinity of the word 'Israel', as in 'U.S.-Israeli domination of the Middle East' or 'the U.S. drive to assure global domination and guarantee security for Israel', and some Leftist who otherwise opposes going to war against Iraq will trot out charges of promoting the *Protocols of the Elders of Zion,* the old czarist forgery that asserted a Jewish plan for world domination."

Presumably, this is what Zunes would call an example of the "latent anti-Semitism which has come to the fore with wildly exaggerated claims of Jewish economic and political power". And that it "is a naive assumption to believe that foreign policy decision making in the US is pluralistic enough so that any one lobbying group ... can have so much influence."

This is hardly the first time that Jews have been in the upper echelons of power, as Benjamin Ginsberg points out in *The Fatal Embrace: Jews and the State,* but there has never been a situation anything like the present. This is how Ginsberg began his book:

"Since the 1960s, Jews have come to wield considerable influence in American economic, cultural, intellectual and political life. Jews played a central role in American finance during the 1980s, and they were among the chief beneficiaries of that decade's corporate mergers and reorganizations. Today, though barely 2 % of the nation's population is Jewish, close to half its billionaires are Jews. The chief executive officers of the three major television networks and the four largest film studios are Jews, as are the owners of the nation's largest newspaper chain and the most influential single newspaper, the New York Times."

That was written in 1993. Today, ten years later, ardently pro-Israel American Jews are in positions of unprecedented influence within the United States and have assumed or been given decision making positions over virtually every segment of our culture and body politic. This is no secret conspiracy. Regular readers of The New York Times business section, which reports the comings and goings of the media tycoons, are certainly aware of it. Is each and every tycoon a pro-Israel zealot? Not necessarily, but when one compares the US media with its European counterparts in their respective coverage of the Israel-Palestine conflict, the extreme bias in favor of Israel on the part of the US media is immediately apparent.

This might explain Nation columnist Eric Alterman's discovery that "Europeans and Americans ... differ profoundly in their views of the Israel/Palestine issue at both the elite and popular levels ... with Americans being far more sympathetic to Israel and the Europeans to the Palestinian cause".

An additional component of Chomsky's analysis is his insistence that it is the US, more than Israel, that is the "rejectionist state", implying that were it not for the US, Israel might long ago have abandoned the West Bank and Gaza to the Palestinians for a mini-state.

Essential to his analysis is the notion that every US administration since that of Eisenhower has attempted to advance

Israel's interests in line with America's global and regional agenda. This is a far more complex issue than Chomsky leads us to believe. Knowledgeable insiders, both critical and supportive of Israel, have described in detail major conflicts that have taken place between US and Israeli administrations over the years in which Israel, thanks to the diligence of its domestic lobby, prevailed.

In particular, Chomsky ignores or misinterprets the efforts made by every US president beginning with Richard Nixon to curb Israel's expansionism, halt its settlement building and obtain its withdrawal from the Occupied Territories.

"What happened to all those nice plans?" asked Israeli journalist and peace activist Uri Avnery.

"Israel's governments ... mobilized the collective power of US Jewry—which dominates Congress and the media to a large degree—against them. Faced by this vigorous opposition, all the presidents—great and small, football players and movie stars—folded one after another."

Gerald Ford, angered that Israel had been reluctant to leave the Sinai following the 1973 war not only suspended aid for six months in 1975 but in March of that year made a speech, backed by Secretary of State Henry Kissinger, that called for a "reassessment" of the US-Israel relationship. Within weeks, AIPAC (American-Israel Public Affairs Committee), Israel's Washington lobby, secured a letter signed by 76 senators confirming their support for Israel, and suggesting that the White House see fit to do the same. The language was tough, the tone almost bullying. Ford backed down.

We need only look at the current Bush presidency to see that this phenomenon is still the rule. In 1991, the same year as Chomsky's talk, Israeli Prime Minister Yitzhak Shamir asked the first Bush administration for $10 billion in loan guarantees in order, he said, to provide for the resettlement of Russian Jews. Bush Sr. had earlier balked at a request from Congress to appropriate an additional $650 million dollars to compensate Israel for sitting out the Gulf War, but gave in when he realized that his veto would be overridden. But now he told Shamir that Israel could have the guarantees only if it would freeze settlement building and promised that no Russian Jews would be resettled in the West Bank.

An angry Shamir refused and called on AIPAC to mobilize Congress and the organized American Jewish community in support of the loan guarantees. A letter, drafted by AIPAC, was signed by more than 240 members of the House demanding that Bush approve them, and 77 senators signed on to supporting legislation.

On September 12, 1991, Jewish lobbyists descended on Washington in such numbers that Bush felt obliged to call a televised press conference in which he complained that "1000 Jewish lobbyists are on Capitol Hill against little old me". It would prove to be his epitaph.

Chomsky pointed to Bush's statement, at the time, as proof that the vaunted Israel lobby was nothing more than "a paper tiger". "It took scarcely more than a raised eyebrow for the lobby to collapse", he told readers of Z Magazine. He could not have been further from the truth.

The next day, Tom Dine, AIPAC's Executive Director, declared that "September 12, 1991, is a day that will live in infamy". Similar comments were uttered by Jewish leaders who accused Bush of provoking anti-Semitism. What was more important, his friends in the mainstream media, like William Safire, George Will and Charles Krauthammer, not only criticized him, they began to find fault with the economy and how he was running the country. It was all downhill from there. Bush's Jewish vote, which had been estimated at 38% in 1988, dropped down to no more than 12%, with some estimates as low as 8%.

Bush's opposition to the loan guarantees was the last straw for the Israel lobby. When he made disparaging comments about Jewish settlements in East Jerusalem in March 1990, AIPAC had begun the attack (briefly halted during the the Gulf War). Dine wrote a critical op-ed in The New York Times and followed that with a vigorous speech to the United Jewish Appeal's Young Leaders Conference. "Brothers and sisters", he told them as they prepared to go out and lobby Congress on the issue, "remember that Israel's friends in this city reside on Capitol Hill." Months later, the loan guarantees were approved, but by then, Bush was dead meat.

Now, jump ahead to last Spring when Bush Jr. forthrightly demanded that Israeli Prime Minister Ariel Sharon withdraw his troops from Jenin, saying "Enough is enough!" It made headlines all over the world, as did his backing down when Sharon refused. What happened? Harsh criticism boomed from within his own party in Congress and from his daddy's old friends in the media. Will associated Dubya with Yasser Arafat and accused Bush of having lost his "moral clarity". The next day, Safire suggested that Bush was "being pushed into a minefield of mistakes" and that he had "become a wavering ally as Israel fights for survival". Junior got the message and within a week declared Sharon to be "a man of peace". Since then, as journalist Robert Fisk and others have noted, Sharon seems to be writing Bush's speeches.

There are some who believe that Bush Jr. and presidents before him made statements critical of Israel for appearances only, to convince the world, and the Arab countries in particular, that the US can be an "honest broker" between the Israelis and the Palestinians. But it is difficult to make a case that any of them would put themselves in a position to be humiliated simply as a cover for US policy.

A better explanation was provided by Stephen Green, whose *Taking Sides: America's Secret Relations with Militant Israel* was the first examination of State Department archives concerning US-Israel relations. Since the Eisenhower administration, wrote Green, in 1984, "Israel, and friends of Israel in America, have determined the broad outlines of US policy in the region. It has been left to American Presidents to implement that policy, with varying degrees of enthusiasm, and to deal with the tactical issues."

An exaggeration, perhaps, but former US Senator James Abourezk (D-South Dakota) echoed Green's words in a speech before the American-Arab Anti-Discrimination Committee last June:

"That is the state of American politics today. The Israeli lobby has put together so much money power that we are daily witnessing US senators and representatives bowing down low to Israel and its US lobby.

"Make no mistake. The votes and bows have nothing to do with the legislators' love for Israel. They have everything to do with the money that is fed into their campaigns by members of the Israeli lobby. My estimate is that at least $6 billion flows from the American Treasury to Israel each year. That money, plus the political support the US gives Israel at the United Nations, is what allows Israel to conduct criminal operations in Palestine with impunity."

That is a reality that has been expressed many times in many forms by ex-members of Congress, usually speaking off the record. It is the reality that Chomsky and those who accept his analysis prefer to ignore.

The problem is not so much that Chomsky has been wrong. He has, after all, been right on many other things, particularly in describing the ways in which the media manipulate the public consciousness to serve the interests of the state. However, by explaining US support for Israel simply as a component of those interests, and ignoring the influence of the Israel lobby in determining that component, he appears to have made a major error that has had measurable consequences. By accepting Chomsky's analysis, the Palestinian solidarity movement has failed to take the only political step that might have weakened the hold of Israel on Congress and the American electorate: namely, challenging the billions of dollars in aid and tax breaks that the US provides Israel on an annual basis.

The questions that beg asking are why his argument has been so eagerly accepted by the movement and why the contrary position put forth by people of considerable stature, such as Edward Said, Ed Herman, Uri Avnery and, more recently, Alexander Cockburn, has been ignored. There appear to be several reasons.

The people who make up the movement, Jews and non-Jews alike, have embraced Chomsky's position because it is the message they want to hear; not feeling obligated to "blame the Jews" is reassuring. The fear of either provoking anti-Semitism or being called an anti-Semite (or a self-hating Jew) has become so ingrained into our culture and body politic that no one, including Chomsky or Zunes, is immune. This is reinforced by constant reminders of the Jewish Holocaust that, by no accident, appear in the movies and in major news media on a regular basis. Chomsky, in particular, has been heavily criticized by the Jewish establishment for decades for his criticism of Israeli policies, even to the point of being "excommunicated", a distinction he shares with the late Hannah Arendt. It may be fair to assume that at some level this history influences Chomsky's analysis.

But the problems of the movement go beyond the fear of invoking anti-Semitism, as Chomsky is aware and correctly noted in *The Fateful Triangle*:

"[T]he American Left and pacifist groups, apart from fringe elements, have quite generally been extremely supportive of

Israel (contrary to many baseless allegations), some passionately
so, and have turned a blind eye to practices that they would be
quick to denounce elsewhere."

The issue of US aid to Israel provides a clear example. During
the Reagan era, there was a major effort launched by the anti-
intervention movement to block a $15 million annual appropri-
ation destined for the Nicaraguan contras. People across the
country were urged to call their congressional representatives
and get them to vote against the measure. That effort was not
only successful; it forced the administration to engage in what
became known as Contragate.

At the time, Israel was receiving the equivalent of that much
money on a daily basis. Now, that amount "officially" is about
$10 million a day and yet no major campaign has ever been
launched to stem that flow or even call the public's attention to
it. When attempts were made they were stymied by the opposition of such key players (at the time) as the American Friends
Service Committee which was anxious, apparently, not to alien-
ate major Jewish contributors. (Recent efforts initiated on the
Internet to "suspend" military aid—but not economic!—until
Israel ends the occupation have gone nowhere.)

The slogans that have been advanced by various sectors of
the Palestinian solidarity movement, such as "End the Occupation", "End Israeli Apartheid", "Zionism Equals Racism" or
"Two States for Two Peoples", while addressing key issues of the
conflict, assume a level of awareness on the part of the
American people for which no evidence exists. Concern for
where their tax dollars are going, particularly at a time of
massive cutbacks in social programs, certainly would have
greater resonance. Initiating a serious campaign to halt aid
would require focusing on the role of Congress and recognition
of the role of the Israel lobby.

Chomsky's evaluation of Israel's position in the Middle East
admittedly contains elements of truth, but nothing sufficient to

explain what former Undersecretary of State George Ball described as America's "passionate attachment" to the Jewish state. However, his attempt to portray the US-Israel relationship as mirroring that of Washington's relations to its client regimes in El Salvador, Guatemala and Nicaragua has no basis in reality.

US involvement in Central America was fairly simple. Arms and training were supplied to military dictatorships in order for their armies and their death squads to suppress the desires of their own citizens for land, civil rights and economic justice, all of which would undermine US corporate interests. This was quite transparent. Does Israel fit into that category? Obviously not. Whatever one may say about Israel, its Jewish majority, at least, enjoys democratic rights.

Also, there were no Salvadoran, Nicaraguan or Guatemalan lobbies of any consequence in Washington to lavish millions of dollars wooing or intimidating members of Congress; no one in the House or Senate from any of those client countries with possible dual loyalties approving multibillion-dollar appropriations on an annual basis; none owning major television networks, radio stations, newspapers or movie studios; and no trade unions or state pension funds investing billions of dollars in their respective economies. The closest thing in the category of national lobbies is that of Miami's Cuban exiles, whose existence and power the left is willing to acknowledge, even though its political clout is minuscule compared with that of Israel's supporters.

What about Chomsky's assertion that Israel is America's cop-on-the-beat in the Middle East? There is, as yet, no record of a single Israeli soldier shedding a drop of blood in behalf of US interests, and there is little likelihood one will be asked to do so in the future. When US presidents have believed that a cop was necessary in the region, US troops were ordered to do the job.

When President Eisenhower believed that US interests were threatened in Lebanon in 1958, he sent in the Marines. In 1991, as mentioned, President Bush not only told Israel to sit on the sidelines, he further angered its military by refusing to allow Vice President Dan Quayle to give the Israeli air force the co-ordinates it demanded in order to take to the air in response to Iraq's Scud attacks. This left the Israeli pilots literally sitting in their planes, waiting for information that never came.

What Chomsky offers as proof of Israel's role as a US gen-darme is the warning that Israel gave Syria not to intervene in King Hussein's war on the Palestine Liberation Organization in Jordan in September 1970.

Clearly this was done primarily to protect Israel's interests. That it also served Washington's agenda was a secondary con-sideration. For Chomsky, it was "another important service" for the US. What Chomsky ignores and most historians fail to mention is another reason that Syria failed to come to the rescue of the Palestinians at the time.

The commander of the Syrian air force, Hafez Al-Assad, had shown little sympathy with the Palestinian cause and was critical of the friendly relations that the PLO enjoyed with the Syrian government under President Atassi. When King Hussein launched his attack, Assad kept his planes on the ground.

Three months later, he staged a coup and installed himself as president. Among his first acts was the imprisonment of hun-dreds of Palestinians and their Syrian supporters. He then pro-ceeded to gut the Syrian-sponsored militia, Al-Saika, and elimi-nate the funds that Syria had been sending to Palestinian militia groups. In the ensuing years, Assad allowed groups opposed to Yasser Arafat to maintain offices and a radio station in Damas-cus, but little else. A year after Israel's invasion of Lebanon, he sponsored a short but bloody intra-Palestinian civil war in Northern Lebanon. This is history that has fallen through the cracks.

How much the presence of Israel has intimidated its weaker Arab neighbors from endangering US interests is at best a matter of conjecture. Certainly, Israel's presence has been used by these reactionary regimes, most of them US allies, as an excuse for suppressing internal opposition movements. (One might argue that the CIA's involvement in the overthrow of Mossadegh in Iran in 1953, and Abdel Karim Kassem in Iraq in 1963, had more of an impact on crushing progress in the region.)

What Israel has provided for the US to their mutual benefit have been a number of joint weapons programs, largely financed by US taxpayers, and the use by the US of military equipment developed by Israeli technicians, not the least of which were the "plows" that were used to bury alive fleeing Iraqi soldiers in the first Gulf War. Since high levels of US aid preceded these weapons programs, it is hard to argue that they form the basis of US support for Israel.

Another argument advanced by Chomsky has been Israel's willingness to serve the US by taking on tasks that past US administrations were unable or unwilling to undertake due to specific US laws or public opinion, such as selling arms to unsavory regimes or training death squads.

That Israel did this at the request of the US is an open question. A comment by Israeli minister Yakov Meridor in Ha'aretz is revealing:

"We shall say to the Americans: Don't compete with us in Taiwan, don't compete with us in South Africa, don't compete with us in the Caribbean area, or in other areas in which we can sell weapons directly and where you can't operate in the open. Give us the opportunity to do this and trust us with the sales of ammunition and hardware."

In fact, there was no time that the US stopped training death squads in Latin America or providing arms, with the exception of Guatemala, where Carter halted US assistance because of massive human rights violations, something that presented no problem for an Israeli military already steeped in such violations. In one case we saw the reverse situation. Israel provided more than 80 percent of El Salvador's weapons before the US moved in.

As for Israel's trade and joint arms projects with South Africa, including the development of nuclear weaponry, that was a natural alliance; two societies that had usurped someone else's land and saw themselves in the same position, "a civilized people surrounded by threatening savages". The relationship became so close that South Africa's Sun City became the resort of choice for vacationing Israelis.

The reason that Israeli officials gave for selling these weapons, when questioned, was it was the only way that Israel could keep its own arms industry functioning. Israel's sales of weaponry to China have drawn criticism from several adminis-trations, but this has been tempered by congressional pressure.

What Israel did benefit from was a blanket of silence from the US anti-intervention movement and anti-apartheid movement, whose leadership was more comfortable criticizing US policies than those of Israel. Whether their behavior was due to their willingness to put Israel's interests first, or whether they were concerned about provoking anti-Semitism, the result was the same.

A protest that I organized in 1985 against Israel's ties to apartheid South Africa and its role as a US surrogate in Central America provides a clear example. When I approached board members of the Nicaraguan Information Center (NIC) in the San Francisco Bay Area and asked for the group's endorsement of the protest, I received no support.

NIC was the main Nicaraguan solidarity group, and despite Israel's long and ugly history, first in aiding Somoza, and at the time of the protest, the contras, the board voted ... well, it couldn't vote not to endorse, so it voted to make "no more endorsements", a position they reversed soon after our rally. NIC's board was almost entirely Jewish.

I fared better with GNIB, the Guatemalan News and Information Bureau, but only after a considerable struggle. At the time, Israel was supplying 98 percent of the weaponry and all of the training to one of the most murderous regimes in modern times. One would think that an organization that claimed to be working in solidarity with the people of Guatemala would not only endorse the rally but be eager to participate.

Apparently, the GNIB board was deeply divided on the issue. Unwilling to accept another refusal, I harassed the board with phone calls until it voted to endorse. Oakland CISPES (Committee in Solidarity with the People of El Salvador) endorsed. The San Francisco chapter declined. (A year earlier, when I had been quoted in the San Francisco Weekly criticizing the influence of the Israel lobby on the Democratic Party, officials from the chapter wrote a letter to the editor claiming that I was provoking "anti-Semitism".) The leading anti-apartheid organizations endorsed the protest but, again, only after lengthy internal debate.

The protest had been organized in response to the refusal of the San Francisco-based Mobilization for Peace, Jobs and Justice (Mobe), a coalition of movement organizations, to include any mention of the Middle East among the demands that it was issuing for a march opposing South African apartheid and US intervention in Central America.

At an organizing meeting for the event, a handful of us asked that a plank calling for "No US Intervention in the Middle East" be added to the demands that had previously been decided. The vote was overwhelmingly against it. A Jewish trade unionist told us that "we could do more for the Palestinians by not mentioning them than by mentioning them", a strange response which mirrored what President Reagan was then saying about ending apartheid in South Africa. We were privately told that if the Middle East was mentioned, "the unions would walk", recognition of the strong support for Israel that exists among the labor bureaucracy.

The timing of the Mobe's refusal was significant. Two and a half years earlier, Israel had invaded Lebanon and its troops still remained there as we met on that evening in San Francisco. And yet, the leaders of the Mobe would not let Tina Naccache, a programmer for Berkeley's KPFA, the only Lebanese in the large union hall, speak in behalf of the demand.

Three years later, the Mobe scheduled another mass march. The Palestinians were in the first full year of their intifada, and it seemed appropriate that a statement calling for an end to Israeli occupation be added to the demands. The organizers, the same ones from 1985, had already decided on what those would be behind closed doors: "No US Intervention in Central America or the Caribbean; End US Support for South African Apartheid; Freeze and Reverse the Nuclear Arms Race; Jobs and Justice, Not War".

This time the Mobe took no chances and canceled a public meeting where our demand could be debated and voted on. An Emergency Coalition for Palestinian Rights was formed in response. A petition was circulated supporting the demand. Close to 3,000 people signed it, including hundreds from the Palestinian community. The Mobe leadership finally agreed to one concession. On the back of its official flyer, where it would be invisible when posted on a wall or tree, was the following sentence:

"Give peace a chance everywhere: The plight of the Palestinian people, as shown by the recent events in the West Bank and Gaza, remind us that we must support human rights everywhere. Let the nations of our world turn from building armies and death machines to spending their energy and resources on improving the quality of life—Peace, Jobs and Justice."

There was no mention of Israel or the atrocities its soldiers were committing. The flyer put out by the unions ignored the subject completely.

Fast forward to February 2002, when a new and smaller version of the Mobe met to plan a march and rally to oppose the US war on Afghanistan. There was a different cast of characters but they produced the same result. The argument was that what was needed was a "broad" coalition, and raising the issue of Palestine would prevent that from happening.

The national movement to oppose the extension of the Iraq war has been no different. As in 1991, at the time of the Gulf War, there were competing large marches, separately organized but with overlapping participants. Despite their other political differences, what the organizers of both marches agreed on was that there would be no mention of the Israel-Palestine conflict in any of the protest literature, even though its connections to the situation in Iraq were being made at virtually every other demonstration taking place throughout the world. The movement's fear of alienating American Jews still holds sway over defending the rights of Palestinians.

Last September, the slogan of "No War on Iraq—Justice for Palestine!" drew close to a half million protesters to Trafalgar Square. The difference was expressed by a Native American leader during the first intifada. "The problem with the movement", he told me, "is that there are too many liberal Zionists."

If there is one event that exposed their influence over the movement, it is what occurred in New York City on June 12, 1982, when 800,000 people gathered in Central Park to call for a freeze on nuclear weapons. Six days earlier, on June 6th, Israel had launched a devastating invasion of Lebanon. Its goal was to destroy the Palestine Liberation Organization then based in that country. Eighty thousand soldiers, backed by massive bombing from the air and from the sea were creating a level of death and destruction that dwarfed what Iraq would later do in Kuwait.

Within a year there would be 20,000 Palestinians and Lebanese dead and tens of thousands more wounded.

And what was the response that day in New York? In recognition of the suffering then taking place in his homeland, a Lebanese man was allowed to sit on the stage, but he would not be introduced, not allowed to say a word. Nor was the subject mentioned by any of the speakers. Israel and its lobby couldn't have asked for anything more.

Twenty-one years later, Ariel Sharon, the architect of that invasion, is Israel's Prime Minister, having been elected for the second time. As I write these lines, pro-Israel zealots within the Bush administration are about to savor their greatest triumph. After all, they have been the driving force for a war that they envision as the first stage in "redrawing the map of the Middle East" with the US-Israel alliance at its fore.

And the left? Rabbi Arthur Waskow, a long-time activist with impeccable credentials, assured the Jewish weekly, Forward, that United for Peace and Justice, organizers of the February 15 anti-war rally in New York, "has done a great deal to make clear it is not involved in anti-Israel rhetoric. From the beginning there was nothing in United for Peace's statements that dealt at all with the Israel-Palestine issue".

But maybe things do move forward.

At the start of June United for Peace and Justice staged a big conference in Chicago attended by hundreds of peace agitators from across the country. Out of that came an action program, approved by the entire assembly, including a "Campaign for Justice for Palestine" and a mandate "to craft a message that will assure broad participation and sensitivity to both the Palestinian and Jewish communities".

There was also a working document, known as the "unity statement", which included this language: "U.S. military involvement is on the rise in Latin America, Africa, and Asia, reflected by increased aid to Colombia's repressive governments, an increase in U.S. troops in the Philippines, and the expansion of a network of military bases stretching from East Africa to South Asia. U.S. political, economic, and military aid is fueling Israel's rise as an unchallengeable regional military power and sustains Israel's illegal occupation of the Palestinian West Bank, Gaza, and East Jerusalem and its denial of equal rights to Palestinians."

Jeffrey Blankfort is the former editor of Middle East Labor Bulletin and currently hosts a radio program on KZYX and KPOO in Mendocino County, Northern California. Thanks to Left Curve which first published this essay.

George Sunderland
Our Vichy Congress

WHAT DOES IT MEAN TO CROSS THE LINE BETWEEN Constitutionally protected activities and openly treasonable behavior?

Probably the emblematic example of this kind of generalized disloyalty to the country of one's birth is the Vichy government of France. Histories of the fall of France, such as William Shirer's *Collapse of the Third Republic*, or Alistair Horne's *To Lose a Battle*, take pains to emphasize that France's military collapse and generally subservient loyalty to German occupation had their source not in military weakness per se but in the profound cynicism, corruption and attenuated loyalty of interwar France's professional class of politicians.

One of the archetypes that reverberates in our extended historical memory is the thoroughly distasteful picture of the dozing, senile Petain, the feral, rat-like Leval and a supporting cast of seedy hack politicians clenching acrid Gauloise cigarettes between tobacco-stained fingers. When Petain spoke of the "duty of loyalty" of France's citizens to a collaborationist regime, the modern reader has no difficulty in calculating that black is white and up is down. Loyalty to France was not the loyalty preached and practiced by the politicians in Vichy. At the end of World War II, many of these politicians found themselves at the end of a rope. What, then, is one to make of our representatives and senators in Congress assembled?

For expressions of sheer groveling subservience to a foreign power, the pronouncements of Laval and Petain pale in comparison with the rhetorical devotion with which certain congressmen have bathed the Israel of Ariel Sharon.

In March, Senator James Inhofe of Oklahoma took the Senate floor and said the September 11 attacks were punishment by

God in response to US policy towards Israel. Asserting that Israel is "entitled" to the West Bank, he also criticized his fellow citizens who counseled the Israelis to use restraint, in effect blaming them for the terrorist attacks of September 11: "One of the reasons I believe the spiritual door was opened for an attack against the United States of America is that the policy of our government has been to ask the Israelis, and demand it with pressure, not to retaliate in a significant way against the terrorist strikes that have been launched against them."

According to this Tornado-Belt St. Augustine, God in effect allowed airliners to be flown into the World Trade Center and the Pentagon because US actions towards Israel offended the Almighty. In other words, the United States was punished because the Bush administration had been insufficiently worshipful towards Israel (the $3 billion annually that Congress squeezes out of the taxpayer as tribute to the Jewish State is apparently not sufficient in the opinion of this self-styled "fiscal conservative"—and in the opinion of the Almighty Himself, Whose inscrutable will Inhofe claims to be able to interpret).

Like Jerry Falwell and Pat Robertson, Inhofe believes America suffered divinely ordained punishment; but the Senator adds a new twist: those 3,000 innocent Americans died, he believes, because their government demonstrated insufficient obeisance to a foreign country. For sheer treacherous Quislingism, Inhofe's statement is hard to top.

But top it we can.

A perusal of the May 6, 2002, Jerusalem Post reveals the following headline: "Visiting Congressmen Advise Israel to Resist US Administration Pressure". The Israeli newspaper chronicles the pilgrimage of a group of Congressional wardheelers to the Promised Land, carrying with them a copy of the resolution of support for the Israeli government that passed Congress by a vote of 352-21 with 29 abstentions. The delegation's leader, Rep. James Saxton of New Jersey, displayed a copy of the resolution to reporters, which he said they wanted to "hand deliver" to the Israeli people. Saxton's enthusiasm for Israel is a matter of long standing, and extends to providing congressional employment to Israeli citizen—and rumored Mossad asset—Yosef Bodansky.

An ironic aspect to this congressional junket is that these are precisely the public officials who routinely suggest that dissent against the Bush administration's conduct of the war in Afghanistan is tantamount to treason.

Senate Minority Leader Tom Daschle's tepid criticism of Bush's policies in March elicited a firestorm of self-righteous indignation from Republicans, and Daschle, duly chastised, slunk offstage.

No criticism of President Bush is warranted, apparently, except where Israel is involved. In that case, one is permitted to travel to foreign countries at taxpayer expense for the purpose of publicly undercutting one's own government's foreign policy. What gives this circumstance added savor is the recollection that Jesse Jackson's erstwhile forays into hostage negotiation in Lebanon and the Balkans met with grumbling from Republicans that Jackson ought to be prosecuted for violating the Logan Act. Again, apparently the Israel exception applies.

A further example of Vichyite subservience is provided by John McCain, adored pet of newspaper editorial boards and in relentless competition with Joseph Lieberman as Conscience of the Senate pro tempore. Addressing the closing plenary session of the American-Israel Public Affairs Committee at the Jefferson Memorial on April 23, 2002, McCain pledged his troth to Sharon's Israel in a manner that would have been denounced as fellow-travelership or useful idiocy had it been Henry Wallace praising the Soviet Union.

Invoking Senator Henry "Scoop" Jackson (the founder, as it were, of congressional Vichyism, a truly odious pork-barreling errand boy of the military industrial complex whose chief contribution to American statecraft was launching the careers of the smoothly sinister Richard Perle and howling militarist Frank Gaffney) McCain described the indissoluble moral bond between the American Republic and the Middle Eastern apartheid state run by an ex-general currently under indictment by a Belgian court for war crimes. Indeed, "To be proudly pro-American and pro-Israeli is not to hold conflicting loyalties. As Scoop understood, it is about defending the principles that both countries hold dear. And I stand before you today, proudly pro-American and pro-Israel." It is notable that McCain produced this effusion at an American national memorial, surrounded by Israeli flags. The Senator apparently thinks that this scene would be so impressive to his Arizona constituents that he put a picture of it on his web site.

Command performances before AIPAC have become standard features in the life of a Washington elected official, like filing FEC reports and hitting on interns. The stylized panegyrics delivered at the annual AIPAC meeting have all the probative value of the Dniepropetrovsk Soviet's birthday greeting to Stalin, because the actual content is unimportant; what is crucial is that the politician in question be seen to be genuflecting before the AIPAC board. In fact, to make things easier, the speeches are sometimes written by an AIPAC employee, with cosmetic changes inserted by a member of the senator's or congressman's own staff.

Of course, there are innumerable lobbies in Washington, from environmental to telecommunications to chiropractic; why is AIPAC different? For one thing, it is a political action committee that lobbies expressly on behalf of a foreign power; the fact that it is exempt from the Foreign Agents' Registration Act is yet another mysterious "Israel exception". For another, it is important not just for the amount of money it gives but for the political punishment it can exact: just ask Chuck Percy or Pete McClosky. Since the mid-1980s, no member of Congress has even tried to take on the lobby directly. As a Senate staffer told this writer, it is the "cold fear" of AIPAC's disfavor that keeps the politicians in line. This scam has been going on for decades.

The main purpose, other than to maintain the flow of weapons and loot to Israel, is to keep Congress's investigatory apparatus turned off. AIPAC appears to be batting a thousand. Lyndon Johnson's decision to cover up the deliberate and protracted Israeli attack on the USS Liberty in June 1967 (which resulted in 34 deaths, almost double the deaths suffered by the crew of the USS Cole) was pointedly not investigated by Congress. Instead, the surviving crew were shamefully bullied into silence by the gargoyle Johnson and his functionaries; those who did break their silence later were reviled by the lobby as delusional anti-Semites.

Likewise, the congressional investigation into the Beirut barracks bombing stuck to the narrow issue of the incompetent US military chain of command, and avoided the wider issue of the Marines' presence as sitting ducks in the middle of Sharon's first war of conquest. A retired officer has asserted that the Mossad had intelligence from informers that the frame of a truck was being reinforced to carry a heavy load of explosives, but chose to keep the intelligence secret. Despite the lobby's claim that the US-Israel relationship is one of mutual intelligence sharing, the real relationship is a starker one: according to old intelligence hands, Israel takes all and gives nothing, even if U.S. lives are at stake.

The way for then-National Security Advisor Bud McFarlane's "opening to Iran" was paved by the fact that Israel was already providing F-4 Phantom spare parts (manufactured in the United States and transported to Israel at American taxpayer expense) to Iran on the sly as a way of counterbalancing Iraq's military power. The extent to which President Reagan's privatized foreign policy used these pre-existing links to pursue the Iranian opening is uncertain. What is certain is that the joint House-Senate investigating committee, chaired by long-time

AIPAC favorite Senator Daniel Inouye of Hawaii, took some pains to steer the investigation away from Israel, so that those links would not be made public in a way that would embarrass our major non-NATO ally. Finally, for a country that loves a good spy mystery—whether it involves Alger Hiss, the Rosenbergs or Robert Hansen, each one eliciting from Capitol Hill cries for an investigation, more polygraphs, increased use of the death penalty, etc., etc.—Congress's deafening silence over the Israeli "art students" saga, particularly after 9/11, is astonishing for those unfamiliar with Congress's reticence about embarrassing Israel. All the more amazing that only two years before, the Hill was in an uproar over the Chinese spy hysteria (the fact that Wen Ho Lee, the apparently falsely accused Los Alamos employee, had been fingered in the columns of manic Zionist and Sharon confidant William Safire supplies an almost O. Henry quality of irony to the tale). The full story of how hundreds of Mossad agents-in-training were literally inundating federal facilities in the year and a half prior to 9/11 may never be known, thanks to a total smothering by the Justice Department, Congress and the major media.

As year chases year, the lobby's power to influence Congress on any issue of importance to Israel grows inexorably stronger. In 1995, coincidentally the year her then-husband became Speaker of the House, Marianne Gingrich was hired by the Israel Export Development Co., Ltd (IEDC) as its vice president for business development. Mrs. Gingrich's interest in Israel began during an eight-day trip to Israel she and her husband made in August 1994 at AIPAC's expense.

Was it a political payoff from a foreign power?

"If I were going to get a political payoff, it would not be for the amount of money I am making", said Mrs. Gingrich, who had no experience in the field. Her salary was $2,500 per month, "plus commissions", the size of which neither she nor anyone connected with the business would reveal.

By an even odder coincidence, the newly minted Speaker Gingrich's foreign policy prescriptions became stridently pro-Israel and bellicosely opposed to the countries that Israel designates as enemies. One of Gingrich's notable forays into diplomacy at the time was his public call for the CIA to overthrow the government of Iran. Someone apparently failed to remind the Speaker that the agency had already engineered an Iranian coup in 1953—and look how well that little enterprise turned out.

Israel's strategy of using its influence on the American political system to turn the US national security apparatus into its own personal attack dog—or Golem—has alienated the United States from much of the Third World, has worsened US ties to Europe amid rancorous insinuations of anti-Semitism, and makes the United States a hated bully. And by cutting off all diplomatic lines of retreat—as Sharon did when he publicly made President Bush, the leader of the Free World, look like an impotent fool—Israel paradoxically forces the United States to draw closer to Israel because there is no thinkable alternative for American politicians than continuing to invest political capital in Israel.

We have now reached the point where there may be no turning back as nuclear Armageddon beckons from the Middle East. Writing recently in The Washington Post, Chris Patten, the European commissioner for external relations, says, "A senior Democratic senator [alas, Patten does not name him] told a visiting European the other day: 'All of us here are members of Likud now.'"

So it has come to this: members of the world's greatest deliberative body, the heirs of Clay, La Follette and Taft, now identify themselves with a radical political movement that grew out of the terrorism of the Judeo-Fascist and Mussolini-admirer Vladimir Jabotinsky; Menachim Begin, co-conspirator in the bombing of the King David Hotel; and Ariel Sharon, the butcher of Sabra and Shatila.

Whether they identify with Sharon's Israel because of crass political advantage, or like those of Senator Inhofe's, because their views are indistinguishable from the delusions of a certifiable lunatic, our Vichy Congress is driving us down the path of a final, fatal clash of civilizations. All Americans, be they old-line conservatives who hate seeing their country hopelessly embroiled in the Old World's perpetual quarrels, or liberals in the honorable anti-imperialist and antimilitarist tradition of William Jennings Bryan, or the apolitical who resent the prospect of becoming an irradiated corpse, must put aside their differences and start loudly and persistently identifying these congressional Likudniki for what they are: Quislings.

George Sunderland is the pen name of a senior congressional staffer.

Kathleen and Bill Christison
The Bush Administration's Dual Loyalties

S INCE THE LONG-FORGOTTEN DAYS WHEN THE STATE Department's Middle East policy was run by a group of so-called Arabists, US policy on Israel and the Arab world has increasingly become the purview of officials well known for tilting towards Israel. From the 1920s roughly to 1990, Arabists, who had a personal history and an educational background in the Arab world and who were accused by supporters of Israel of being totally biased towards Arab interests, held sway at the State Department. Despite having limited power in the policy-making circles of any administration, they helped maintain some semblance of US balance by keeping policy from tipping over totally towards Israel. But Arabists have been steadily replaced by their exact opposites, what some observers are calling Israelists, and policymaking circles throughout government now no longer even make a pretense of exhibiting balance between Israeli and Arab, particularly on Palestinian interests.

In the Clinton administration, the three most senior State Department officials dealing with the Palestinian-Israeli peace process were all partisans of Israel to one degree or another. All had lived at least for brief periods in Israel and maintained ties with Israel while in office, occasionally vacationing there. One of these officials had worked both as a pro-Israel lobbyist and as director of a pro-Israel think tank in Washington before taking a position in the Clinton administration from which he helped make policy on Palestinian-Israeli issues. Another has headed the pro-Israel think tank since leaving government.

The link between active promoters of Israeli interests and policymaking circles is stronger by several orders of magnitude in the Bush administration, which is peppered with people who have long records of activism on behalf of Israel in the United

States, of policy advocacy in Israel, and of promoting an agenda for Israel often at odds with existing US policy. These people, who can fairly be called Israeli loyalists, are now at all levels of government, from desk officers at the Defense Department to the deputy secretary level at both State and Defense, as well as on the National Security Council staff and in the vice president's office.

We still tiptoe around putting a name to this phenomenon. We write articles about the neo-conservatives' agenda on US-Israeli relations and imply that in the neo-con universe there is little light between the two countries. We talk openly about the Israeli bias in the US media. We make wry jokes about Congress being "Israeli-occupied territory". But we never pronounce the particular words that best describe the real meaning of those observations and wry remarks. It's time, however, that we say the words out loud and deal with what they really signify.

Dual loyalties. The issue we are dealing with in the Bush administration is dual loyalties—the double allegiance of those myriad officials at high and middle levels who cannot distinguish US interests from Israeli interests, who baldly promote the supposed identity of interests between the United States and Israel, who spent their early careers giving policy advice to right-wing Israeli governments and now give the identical advice to a right-wing US government, and who, one suspects, are so wrapped up in their concern for the fate of Israel that they honestly do not know whether their own passion about advancing the US imperium is motivated primarily by America-first patriotism or is governed first and foremost by a desire to secure Israel's safety and predominance in the Middle East through the advancement of the US imperium.

'Dual loyalties' has always been one of those red flags posted around the subject of Israel and the Arab-Israeli conflict, something that induces horrified gasps and rapid heartbeats because of its implication of Jewish disloyalty to the United States and the common assumption that anyone who would speak such a canard is ipso facto an anti-Semite. (We have a Jewish friend who is not bothered by the term in the least, who believes that US and Israeli interests should be identical and sees it as perfectly natural for American Jews to feel as much loyalty to Israel as they do to the United States. But this is clearly not the usual reaction when the subject of dual loyalties arises.)

Although much has been written about the neo-cons who dot the Bush administration, the treatment of their ties to Israel has generally been very delicate. Although much has come to light recently about the fact that ridding Iraq both of its leader and of its weapons inventory has been on the neo-con agenda since long before there was a Bush administration, little has been said about the link between this goal and the neo-cons' overriding desire to provide greater security for Israel. But an examination of the cast of characters in Bush administration policymaking circles reveals a startlingly pervasive network of pro-Israel activists, and an examination of the neo-cons' voluminous written record shows that Israel comes up constantly as a neo-con reference point, always mentioned with the United States as the beneficiary of a recommended policy, always linked with the United States when national interests are at issue.

The Begats

First to the cast of characters. Beneath cabinet level, the list of pro-Israel neo-cons who are either policy functionaries themselves or advise policymakers from perches just on the edges of government reads like the old biblical "begats". Deputy Secretary of Defense Paul Wolfowitz leads the pack. He was a protege of Richard Perle, who headed the prominent Pentagon advisory body the Defense Policy Board until allegations of financial impropriety caused DoD Secretary Rumsfeld to demote him from the chair of the Board. Many of today's neo-cons, including Perle, are the intellectual progeny of the late Senator Henry "Scoop" Jackson, a hawk and one of Israel's most strident congressional supporters in the 1970s.

Wolfowitz in turn is the mentor of Lewis "Scooter" Libby, now Vice President Cheney's chief of staff, who was first a student of Wolfowitz and later a subordinate during the 1980s in both the State and the Defense Departments. Another Perle protege is Douglas Feith, who is currently undersecretary of defense for policy, the department's number-three man, and has worked closely with Perle both as a lobbyist for Turkey and in co-authoring strategy papers for right-wing Israeli governments. Assistant Secretaries Peter Rodman and Dov Zachkeim, old hands from the Reagan administration when the neo-cons first flourished, fill out the subcabinet ranks at Defense. At lower levels, the Israel and the Syria/Lebanon desk officers at Defense are imports from the Washington Institute for Near East Policy, a think tank spun off from the pro-Israel lobby organization, AIPAC.

Neo-cons have not made many inroads at the State Department, except for John Bolton, an American Enterprise Institute hawk and Israeli proponent who is said to have been forced on a reluctant Colin Powell as undersecretary for arms control. Bolton's special assistant is David Wurmser, who wrote and/or co-authored with Perle and Feith at least two strategy papers for Israeli Prime Minister Netanyahu in 1996. Wurmser's wife, Meyrav Wurmser, is a co-founder of the media-watch website MEMRI (Middle East Media Research Institute), which is run by retired Israeli military and intelligence officers and specializes in translating and widely circulating Arab media and statements by Arab leaders. An investigation by the Guardian of London found that MEMRI's translations are skewed by being highly selective. Although it assiduously trans-lates and circulates the most extreme of Arab statements, it ignores moderate Arab commentary and extremist Hebrew statements.

In the vice president's office, Cheney has established his own personal national security staff, run by aides known to be very pro-Israel. The deputy director of the staff, John Hannah, is a former fellow of the Israeli-oriented Washington Institute. On the National Security Council staff, the newly appointed director of Middle East affairs is Elliott Abrams, who came to prominence after pleading guilty to withholding information from Congress during the Iran-contra scandal (and was pardoned by President Bush the elder) and who has long been a vocal proponent of right-wing Israeli positions. Putting him in a key policy-making position on the Palestinian-Israeli conflict is like entrusting the henhouse to a fox. Abrams is kin of Norman Podhoretz, former editor of Commentary and one of the most hysterical fanatics for Israel in American public life.

Pro-Israel activists with close links to the administration are also busy in the information arena inside and outside government. The head of Radio Liberty, a Cold War propaganda holdover now converted to service in the "war on terror", is Thomas Dine, who was the very active head of AIPAC throughout most of the Reagan and the Bush-41 administrations. Elsewhere on the periphery, William Kristol, son of neo-con originals Irving Kristol and Gertrude Himmelfarb, is closely linked to the administration's pro-Israel coterie and serves as its cheerleader through the Rupert Murdoch-owned magazine that he edits, The Weekly Standard. Some of Bush's speechwriters, including David Frum, who coined the term "axis of evil" for Bush's state-of-the-union address but was forced to resign when his wife publicly bragged about his stylistic prowess, have come from The Weekly Standard. Frank Gaffney, another Jackson and Perle protege and Reagan administration Defense official, puts his pro-Israel oar in from his think tank, the Center for Security

Policy, and through frequent media appearances and regular columns in the Washington Times.

Such is the incestuous nature of the proliferating boards and think tanks, whose membership lists are more or less identical and totally interchangeable. Several scholars at the American Enterprise Institute, including former Reagan UN ambassador and long-time supporter of the Israeli right wing Jeane Kirkpatrick, make their pro-Israel views known vocally from the sidelines and occupy positions on other boards. Probably the most important organization, in terms of its influence on Bush administration policy formulation, is the Jewish Institute for National Security Affairs (JINSA). Formed after the 1973 Arab-Israeli war specifically to bring Israel's security concerns to the attention of US policymakers and concentrating also on broad defense issues, the extremely hawkish, right-wing JINSA has always had a high-powered board able to place its members inside conservative US administrations. Cheney, Bolton and Feith were members until they entered the Bush administration. Several lower level JINSA functionaries are now working in the Defense Department. Perle is still a member, as are Kirkpatrick, former CIA director and leading Iraq war hawk James Woolsey and old-time rabid pro-Israel types like Eugene Rostow and Michael Ledeen. Both JINSA and Gaffney's Center for Security Policy are heavily underwritten by Irving Moskowitz, a right-wing American Zionist, California business magnate (his money comes from bingo parlors) and JINSA board member who has lavishly financed the establishment of several religious settlements in Arab East Jerusalem.

By Their Own Testimony

Most of the neo-cons now in government have left a long paper trail giving clear evidence of their rabidly right-wing pro-Israel, and rabidly anti-Palestinian, sentiments. Whether being pro-Israel, even pro right-wing Israel, constitutes having dual loyalties, that is, a desire to further Israel's interests that equals or exceeds the desire to further US interests, is obviously not easy to determine, but the record gives some clues.

Wolfowitz himself has been circumspect in public, writing primarily about broader strategic issues rather than about Israel specifically or even the Middle East, but it is clear that at bottom Israel is a major interest and may be the principal reason for his near obsession with the effort, of which he is the primary spearhead, to dump Saddam Hussein, remake the Iraqi government in an American image and then further redraw the Middle East map by accomplishing the same goals in Syria, Iran and perhaps other countries. Profiles of Wolfowitz paint him as having two distinct aspects: one obsessively bent on advancing US dominance throughout the world, ruthless and uncompromising, seriously prepared to "end states", as he once put it, that support terrorism in any way, a velociraptor in the words of one former colleague cited in the Economist; the other a softer aspect, which shows him to be a soft-spoken political moralist, an ardent democrat, even a bleeding heart on social issues, and desirous for purely moral and humanitarian reasons of modernizing and democratizing the Islamic world.

But his interest in Israel always crops up. Even profiles that downplay his attachment to Israel nonetheless always mention the influence the Holocaust, in which several of his family perished, has had on his thinking. One source inside the administration has described him frankly as "over-the-top crazy when it comes to Israel". Although this probably accurately describes most of the rest of the neo-con coterie, Wolfowitz is actually more complex and nuanced than this. A New York Times Magazine profile by the Times' Bill Keller cites critics who say that "Israel exercises a powerful gravitational pull on the man" and notes that as a teenager Wolfowitz lived in Israel during his mathematician father's sabbatical semester there. His sister is married to an Israeli. Keller even somewhat reluctantly acknowledges the accuracy of one characterization of Wolfowitz as "Israel-centric". But Keller goes through considerable contortions to shun what he calls "the offensive suggestion of dual loyalty" and in the process makes one wonder if he is protesting too much. Keller concludes that Wolfowitz is less animated by the security of Israel than by the promise of a more moderate Islam. He cites as evidence Wolfowitz's admiration for Egyptian President Anwar Sadat for making peace with Israel, and also draws on a former Wolfowitz subordinate who says that "as a moral man, he might have found Israel the heart of the Middle East story. But as a policy maker, Turkey and the gulf and Egypt didn't loom any less large for him".

These remarks are revealing. Anyone not so fearful of broaching the issue of dual loyalties might at least have raised the suggestion that Wolfowitz's real concern may indeed be to ensure Israel's security. Otherwise, why does his overriding interest seem to be reinventing Anwar Sadats throughout the Middle East by transforming the Arab and Muslim worlds and thereby making life safer for Israel? Why his passion for fighting a pre-emptive war against Iraq when there are critical areas totally apart from the Middle East and myriad other broad strategic issues that any deputy secretary of defense should be thinking about just as much? His current interest in Turkey, which is shared by the other neo-cons, some of whom have served as lobbyists for Turkey, seems also to be directed at securing Israel's place in the region; there seems little reason for particular interest in this moderate Islamic, non-Arab country, other than that it is a moderate Islamic but non-Arab neighbor of Israel.

Furthermore, the notion suggested by the Wolfowitz subordinate that any moral man would obviously look to Israel as the "heart of the Middle East story" is itself an Israel-centered idea: the assumption that Israel is a moral state, always pursuing moral policies, and that any moral person would naturally attach himself to Israel automatically presumes that there is an identity of interests between the United States and Israel; only those who assume such a complete coincidence of interests accept the notion that Israel is, across the board, a moral state.

Others among the neo-con policymakers have been more direct and open in expressing their pro-Israel views. Douglas Feith has been the most prolific of the group, with a two-decade-long record of policy papers, many co-authored with Perle, propounding a strongly anti-Palestinian, pro-Likud view. He views the Palestinians as not constituting a legitimate national group, believes that the West Bank and Gaza belong to Israel by right, and has long advocated that the US abandon any mediating effort altogether and particularly foreswear the land-for-peace formula.

In 1996, Feith, Perle and both David and Meyrav Wurmser were among the authors of a policy paper issued by an Israeli think tank and written for newly elected Israeli Prime Minister Netanyahu that urged Israel to make a "clean break" from pursuit of the peace process, particularly its land-for-peace aspects, which the authors regarded as a prescription for Israel's annihilation. Arabs must rather accept a "peace-for-peace" formula through unconditional acceptance of Israel's rights, including its territorial rights in the Occupied Territories. The paper advocated that Israel "engage every possible energy on rebuilding Zionism" by disengaging from economic and political dependence on the US while maintaining a more "mature", self-reliant partnership with the US not focused "narrowly on territorial disputes". Greater self-reliance would, these freelance policymakers told Netanyahu, give Israel "greater freedom of action and remove a significant lever of pressure [i.e., US pressure] used against it in the past".

The paper advocated, even as far back as 1996, containment of the threat against Israel by working closely with Turkey, as well as with Jordan, apparently regarded as the only reliably moderate Arab regime. Jordan had become attractive for these strategists because it was at the time working with opposition elements in Iraq to re-establish a Hashemite monarchy there that would have been allied by blood lines and political leanings to the Hashemite throne in Jordan. The paper's authors saw the principal threat to Israel coming, we should not be surprised to discover now, from Iraq and Syria and advised that focusing on the removal of Saddam Hussein would kill two birds with one stone by also thwarting Syria's regional ambitions. In what amounts to a prelude to the neo-cons' principal policy thrust in the Bush administration, the paper spoke frankly of Israel's interest in overturning the Iraqi leadership and replacing it with a malleable monarchy. Referring to Saddam Hussein's ouster as "an important Israeli strategic objective" the paper observed that "Iraq's future could affect the strategic balance in the Middle East profoundly", meaning give Israel unquestioned predominance in the region. The authors urged therefore that Israel support the Hashemites in their "efforts to redefine Iraq".

In a much longer policy document written at about the same time for the same Israeli think tank, David Wurmser repeatedly linked the US and Israel when talking about national interests in the Middle East. The "battle to dominate and define Iraq", he wrote "is, by extension, the battle to dominate the balance of power in the Levant over the long run", and "the United States and Israel" can fight this battle together. Repeated references to US and Israeli strategic policy, pitted against a "Saudi-Iraqi-Syrian-Iranian-PLO axis", and to strategic moves that establish a balance of power in which the United States and Israel are ascendant, in alliance with Turkey and Jordan, betray a thought process that cannot separate US from Israeli interests.

Perle gave further impetus to this thrust when six years later, in September 2002, he gave a briefing for Pentagon officials that included a slide depicting a recommended strategic goal for the US in the Middle East: all of Palestine as Israel, Jordan as

Palestine, and Iraq as the Hashemite kingdom. Secretary of Defense Rumsfeld seems to have taken this aboard, since he spoke at about the same time of the West Bank and Gaza as the "so-called occupied territories", effectively turning all of Palestine into Israel.

Elliott Abrams is another unabashed supporter of the Israeli right, now bringing his links with Israel into the service of US policymaking on Palestinian-Israeli issues. The neo-con community crowed about Abrams' appointment as Middle East director on the NSC staff (where this Iran-contra criminal had already been working since mid-2001, badly miscast as the director for, of all things, democracy and human rights). The Weekly Standard's Fred Barnes hailed his appointment as a decisive move that neatly cocked a snook at the pro-Palestinian wimps at the State Department. Accurately characterizing Abrams as "more pro-Israel, less solicitous of Palestinians" than the State Department and strongly opposed to the Palestinian-Israeli peace process, Barnes gloated that the Abrams triumph signaled that the White House would not cede control of Middle East policy to Colin Powell and the "foreign service bureaucrats". Abrams came to the post after a year in which it had effectively been left vacant. His predecessor, Zalmay Khalilzad, had been serving concurrently as Bush's personal representative to Afghanistan since the fall of the Taliban and had devoted little time to the NSC job, but several attempts to appoint a successor early this year were vetoed by neo-con hawks who felt the appointees were not devoted enough to Israel.

Although Abrams has no particular Middle East expertise, he has managed to insert himself in the Middle East debate repeatedly over the years. He has a family interest in propounding a pro-Israel view; he is the son-in-law of Norman Podhoretz, one of the original neo-cons and a long-time strident supporter of right-wing Israeli causes as editor of Commentary magazine, and Midge Decter, a frequent right-wing commentator. Abrams has written a good deal on the Palestinian-Israeli conflict, opposing US mediation and any effort to press for Israeli concessions. In an article published in advance of the 2000 elections, he propounded a rationale for a US missile defense system, and a foreign policy agenda in general, geared almost entirely toward ensuring Israel's security. "It is a simple fact", he wrote, that the possession of missiles and weapons of mass destruction by Iraq and Iran vastly increases Israel's vulnerability, and this threat would be greatly diminished if the US provided a missile shield and brought about the demise of Saddam Hussein. He concluded with a wholehearted assertion of the identity of US and Israeli interests: "The next decade will present enormous opportunities to advance American interests in the Middle East [by] boldly asserting our support of our friends"—that is, of course, Israel. Many of the fundamental negotiating issues critical to Israel, he said, are also critical to US policy in the region and "require the United States to defend its interests and allies" rather than giving in to Palestinian demands.

Neo-cons in the Henhouse

The neo-con strategy papers half a dozen years ago were dotted with concepts like "redefining Iraq", "redrawing the map of the Middle East", "nurturing alternatives to Arafat", all of which have become familiar parts of the Bush administration's diplomatic lingo. Objectives laid out in these papers as important strategic goals for Israel (including the ouster of Saddam Hussein, the strategic transformation of the entire Middle East, the death of the Palestinian-Israeli peace process, regime change wherever the US and Israel don't happen to like the existing government, the abandonment of any effort to forge a comprehensive Arab-Israeli peace or even a narrower Palestinian-Israeli peace) have now become, under the guidance of this group of pro-Israel neo-cons, important strategic goals for the United

States. The enthusiasm with which senior administration officials like Bush himself, Cheney and Rumsfeld have adopted strategic themes originally defined for Israel's guidance (doing so in many cases well before September 11 and the so-called war on terror) testifies to the persuasiveness of a neo-con philosophy focused narrowly on Israel and the pervasiveness of the network throughout policymaking councils.

Does all this add up to dual loyalties to Israel and the United States? Many would still contend indignantly that it does not, and that it is anti-Semitic to suggest such a thing. In fact, zealous advocacy of Israel's causes may be just that: zealotry, an emotional connection to Israel that still leaves room for primary loyalty to the United States. And affection for Israel is not in any case a sentiment limited to Jews. But passion and emotion (and, as George Washington wisely advised, a passionate attachment to any country) have no place in foreign policy formulation, and it is mere hair-splitting to suggest that a passionate attachment to another country is not loyalty to that country. Zealotry clouds judgment, and emotion should never be the basis for policy-making.

Zealotry can lead to extreme actions to sustain policies, as is apparently occurring in the Rumsfeld-Wolfowitz-Feith Defense Department. People knowledgeable of the intelligence community have said that the CIA was under tremendous pressure to produce intelligence more supportive of war with Iraq (as one former CIA official put it, "to support policies that have already been adopted"). Key Defense Department officials, including Feith, are said to have attempted to make the case for pre-emptive war by producing their own unverified intelligence. Wolfowitz betrayed his lack of concern for real evidence when, in answer to a question about where the evidence is for Iraq's possession of weapons of mass destruction, he replied, "It's like the judge said about pornography. I can't define it, but I will know it when I see it."

Zealotry can also lead to a myopic focus on the wrong issues in a conflict or crisis, as is occurring among all Bush policymakers with regard to the Palestinian-Israeli conflict. The administration's obsessive focus on deposing Yasser Arafat, a policy suggested by the neo-cons years before Bush came to office, is a dodge and a diversion that merely perpetuates the conflict by failing to address its real roots.

Advocates of this policy fail or refuse to see that, however unappealing the Palestinian leadership, it is not the cause of the conflict, and "regime change" among the Palestinians will do nothing to end the violence. The administration's refusal to engage in any mediation process that might produce a stable, equitable peace, also a neo-con strategy based on the paranoid belief that any peace involving territorial compromise will spell the annihilation of Israel, will also merely prolong the violence.

Zealotry produces blindness: the zealous effort to pursue Israel's right-wing agenda has blinded the dual loyalists in the administration to the true face of Israel as occupier, to any concern for justice or equity and any consideration that interests other than Israel's are involved, and indeed to any pragmatic consideration that continued unquestioning accommodation of Israel, far from bringing an end to violence, will actually lead to its tragic escalation and to increased terrorism against both the United States and Israel.

What does it matter, in the end, if these men split their loyalties between the United States and Israel? Apart from the evidence of the policy distortions that arise from zealotry, one need only ask whether it can be mere coincidence that most of those in the Bush administration who strongly promoted "regime change" in Iraq are also those who most strongly support the policies of the Israeli right wing. Can it be mere coincidence, for example, that Vice President Cheney, the leading senior-level proponent of "regime change" in Iraq, repudiated that same option for all the right reasons in the immediate aftermath of the

Gulf War in 1991? He was defense secretary at the time, and in an interview with The New York Times on April 13, 1991, he said:

"If you're going to go in and try to topple Saddam Hussein, you have to go to Baghdad. Once you've got Baghdad, it's not clear what you will do with it. It's not clear what kind of government you would put in place of the one that's currently there now. Is it going to be a Shia regime, a Sunni regime or a Kurdish regime? Or one that tilts toward the Ba'athists, or one that tilts toward the Islamic fundamentalists. How much credibility is that government going to have if it's set up by the United States military when it's there? How long does the United States military have to stay to protect the people that sign on for the government, and what happens to it once we leave?"

Since Cheney clearly changed his mind between 1991 and 2001, is it not legitimate to ask why, and whether Israel might have a greater influence over US foreign policy now than it had in 1991? After all, notwithstanding his wisdom in rejecting an expansion of the war on Iraq a decade ago, Cheney was just as interested in promoting US imperialism and was at that same moment in the early 1990s outlining a plan for world domination by the United States, one that did not include conquering Iraq at any point along the way. The only new ingredient in the mix that induced Cheney to begin the march to US world domination by conquering Iraq is the presence in the Bush-Cheney administration of a bevy of aggressive right-wing neo-con hawks who have long backed the Jewish fundamentalists of Israel's own right wing and who have been advocating some move on Iraq for at least the last half-dozen years.

The suggestion that the war with Iraq was planned at Israel's behest, or at the instigation of policymakers whose main motivation is trying to create a secure environment for Israel, is believed by many Israeli analysts. The Israeli commentator Akiva Eldar observed frankly in a Ha'aretz column that Perle, Feith and their fellow strategists "are walking a fine line between their loyalty to American governments and Israeli interests". The suggestion of dual loyalties is not a verboten subject in the Israeli press, as it is in the United States. The peace activist Uri Avnery, who knows Israeli Prime Minister Sharon well, has written that Sharon has long planned grandiose schemes for restructuring the Middle East and that "the winds blowing now in Washington remind me of Sharon. I have absolutely no proof that the Bushies got their ideas from him. But the style is the same."

The dual loyalists in the Bush administration have given added impetus to the growth of a messianic strain of Christian fundamentalism that has allied itself with Israel in preparation for the so-called End of Days. These fundamentalists see Israel's domination over all of Palestine as a necessary step towards fulfillment of the biblical Millennium, consider any Israeli relinquishment of territory in Palestine as a sacrilege, and view warfare between Jews and Arabs as a divinely ordained prelude to Armageddon. These right-wing Christian extremists have a profound influence on Bush and his administration, with the result that the Jewish fundamentalists working for the perpetuation of Israel's domination in Palestine and the Christian fundamentalists working for the Millennium reinforce each other's policies in administration councils. The Armageddon that Christian Zionists seem to be actively promoting (and that Israeli loyalists inside the administration have tactically allied themselves with) raises the prospect of an apocalyptic Christian-Islamic war. The neo-cons seem unconcerned, and Bush's occasional pro forma remonstrations against blaming all Islam for the sins of Islamic extremists do nothing to make this prospect less likely.

These two strains of Jewish and Christian fundamentalism have dovetailed into an agenda for a vast imperial project to restructure the Middle East, all further reinforced by the happy coincidence of great oil resources up for grabs and a president and vice president heavily invested in oil. All of these incentives (the dual loyalties of an extensive network of policymakers allied with Israel, the influence of a fanatical wing of Christian fundamentalists and oil) probably factor in more or less equally to the administration's calculations on the Palestinian-Israeli situation and on war with Iraq. Neither Christian fundamentalist support for Israel nor oil calculations would carry the weight in administration councils that they have without the pivotal input of those Israel loyalists. This is where loyalty to Israel by government officials colors and influences US policymaking in ways that are extremely dangerous.

Kathleen Christison worked in the CIA, retiring in 1979. She is the author of Perceptions of Palestine, *and also* The Wound of Dispossession.
Bill Christison joined the CIA in 1950 and served on the analysis side of the Agency for 25 years. Before he retired in 1979 he was director of the CIA's Office of Regional and Political Analysis.

Yigal Bronner
A Journey to Beit Jalla

THE SKY IS OVERCAST, AND IT BEGINS TO DRIZZLE ON THE hills surrounding Bethlehem as we arrive at the mound blocking the entrance to the village of Beit Jalla. We drive slowly—a convoy of about a hundred cars and four trucks, all loaded with food and medicine—and then come to a halt. The people of Beit Jalla have been under curfew for the last month, with no end in sight. Now, for the first time in several days, the curfew has been lifted for a few hours, allowing them to stock up supplies (not that the shops in the village have much to offer). Several dozen residents decide to spend this precious time on coming to the roadblock in order to welcome us.

We shake hands and embrace, and then get down to work. The food in the cars is unloaded and passed over the mound to a truck waiting on the other side. Several boxes full of medicine—urgently needed in a hospital for the mentally ill—pass hands as well. Three of the trucks continue to other destinations (through a nearby road, controlled by the army), to villages and refugee camps in the Bethlehem area whose situation is even worse than Beit Jalla's.

Meanwhile, as in similar convoys organized by Ta'ayush, an Arab-Jewish group that combines humanitarian aid with political action, a gathering is organized. The Mayor of Beit Jalla is the first speaker. I listen to his description of life under curfew and constant siege as I pass through the crowd. I am looking for the parents of Laith, a nine-year-old boy from Beit Jalla. A few months ago, during a previous round of violence, Laith was smuggled out of his enclosed village by friends, and enjoyed a picnic and a visit to a theme-park in Israel. For one day he was like any other kid, free to run outside and play. This is how I got to know and like him; my family had joined him on his one day of freedom, and my six-year-old son Amos was one of his play-mates.

Now I get to meet his parents, a charming couple. It is an emotional moment. For a brief while we have what resembles a normal conversation among parents. They inquire about Amos, I about Laith. But Laith's childhood is by no means normal. He has been confined to his home for four weeks now, without a single breath of fresh air. Even now, his parents don't allow him out. Too risky. They left him with his aunt, and must soon return for another unknown period of house-arrest. We part with the hope of meeting soon, perhaps under better circum-stances. I try to imagine my son, Amos, in Laith's situation, and find it hard to do. What do you tell a boy his age? How does one explain the need to stay at home? To be patient? What does he think when he sees soldiers roaming the village streets, impos-ing curfew and taking away his freedom?

Speaking of soldiers, they surround us from all sides. Yuri, one of the convoy's organizers is now speaking and addressing the military. He tells the soldiers that they are unwelcome here. He urges them to leave and return one day as guests rather than occupiers and colonizers, and wishes them a safe trip home. He tells them about the misery they are inflicting on the Palestinian civilians. About the hunger and poverty. About the feeling of the farmer who helplessly sees his crops rotting, unable to tend to them. Yuri is followed by Liora. She speaks of the Palestinian women—whose husbands have been detained by the army, and who are now single mothers caring for their children—as the true victims and heroines of this war.

The soldiers stand around us, revealing no emotion. I don't know what they are thinking. But it is clear they wish to be seen as part of our event. By allowing humanitarian aid to pass, they hope to prove that they are "the most humanitarian army in the world". One of them is even documenting the happening with a video-camera, presumably for PR purposes. Just a fortnight ago, the army spokesperson used footage of a similar food convoy headed for the devastated Jenin camp as proof of the humane nature of the Israeli troops (who were meanwhile bulldozing homes on their inhabitants). What the spokesman neglected to mention was that the army stopped the thirty-plus trucks on route to Jenin, despite its promise to let them through, and allowed only a trickle of supplies to pass.

With this recent bitter experience in mind, we are determined not to leave Beit Jalla until we are certain that the trucks have passed all of the military checkpoints. When news arrives from the drivers that they have reached their destination, we begin to wrap things up. We part from our hosts who must hurry home before the curfew is re-imposed, and send the long convoy of cars back to Israel. A few of us remain to wait for the returning truck-drivers. As it turns out, though, our day's adventures are not quite over.

On the way back from Bethlehem, the Israeli military stops one of the empty trucks. Four armored vehicles surround it, a tank points its cannon at it, and the soldiers aim guns at the driver and force him out. We call the driver on the mobile phone; he sounds afraid. The soldiers who gave the truck its entry-permission at the checkpoint promise to release it, but there seems to be a communication problem between them and the troops in Bethlehem.

The minutes go by. It is now late afternoon; the sun is about to set. The truck has not yet been released, and we stand waiting, talking with the driver every few minutes to calm him down. It is cold. But, as we try to warm ourselves, we get another chilling glimpse of the occupation. A small army pickup arrives at the checkpoint with three Palestinians laying in the back. They are in their fifties; their arms and legs are tightly tied, and their eyes are covered. It is quite obvious that they are not on the top of the army's most-wanted list, for they are left unattended. The army base is just around the corner, but no one seems in a hurry to take them in and interrogate them. They simply lay like cattle.

We approach the soldiers and ask them at least to uncover the detainees' eyes. They refuse. An argument ensues, in which the soldiers insist that their mode of action is the most humane. Nonetheless, they prohibit us from photographing the men. After some discussion, they allow us to give them water and cigarettes. We catch a brief word with them. They are from the Deheisha refugee camp. They have no idea where they are now. I don't know why they were arrested. But being a Palestinian man these days automatically makes you suspect, and the most trivial actions such as leaving your home turns you into a criminal.

At last, the truck arrives and we embrace the drivers, the true heroes of the day. We learn that while passing through Bethlehem a large group of residents desperately jumped on top of one truck, grabbing whatever they could. "They were not thieves", the driver, a Palestinian citizen of Israel, explains, "they were simply hungry. One old lady ran after us for a kilometer just to get one pack of rice. I saw very difficult sights. It is an altogether different world there, on the other side of the army checkpoint." We exchange a few more stories, take a photo next to the empty truck, and leave for Jerusalem. As we leave, the three men are still laying in the military pickup truck, tied and blindfolded.

Four cars and one truck drive quickly on the empty road. As the beautiful hills of Bethlehem turn to dusk, we hit the last army checkpoint. The soldiers manning it insist on stopping the Palestinians among us. They are, after all, Arabs. They take away their Israeli IDs for "inspection" which seems to go on forever. They tell us that they have called the police to make sure their "record is clean". We wait together. Another hour passes. It is dark and the wind is freezing. Finally, we decide to protest. Two of us park our cars so as to block traffic to and from the nearby settlement, insisting that if we are not allowed to travel, neither will the settlers. This stirs some commotion. The officer in charge arrives, IDs are returned and we are free to go. We learn that the police had approved our entry a while ago but the soldiers wanted to keep us waiting longer, for the fun of it.

I arrive home a bit after seven. Galila is putting the kids to bed. I kiss Amos and tell him I met Laith's parents, and that they say hi. I tell him some but not all of what I experienced. I put him and my toddler-daughter Naomi to sleep. Then I pause to think. I know I saw only the surface, had only a tiny glimpse of what is really going on in occupied Palestine. I haven't seen the really devastating scenes of Jenin and Nablus. But what I saw, heard and experienced—the child confined to his home for a month, the old lady running after the food-truck, the men laying on the floor of the army vehicle, the soldiers humiliating my Palestinian friends at the roadblock—all that was quite educational. It allowed me to understand that what Israel has been destroying in Palestine is everything but the infrastructure of terrorism. It has been destroying the agricultural, educational, medical and road infrastructure; it has been eroding goodwill and undermining whatever is left of the Palestinian desire for peace. It has been sowing hunger, poverty, humiliation and hatred, all of which serve only to fortify the infrastructure of terrorism. I go to sleep thinking of Amos and Laith, hoping that they can somehow grow up as friends.

Yigal Bronner teaches South Asian literature at Tel Aviv University and is a member of Ta'ayush. For more information on Ta'ayush—Arab-Jewish Partnership—visit HTTP://TAAYUSH.TRIPOD.COM *He recently spent four weeks in military prison for refusing to serve as a reservist in the IDF in the Occupied Territories.*

Edward Said
Dignity, Solidarity and The Penal Colony

ASIDE FROM THE OBVIOUS PHYSICAL DISCOMFORTS, being ill for a long period of time fills the spirit with a terrible feeling of helplessness, but also with periods of analytic lucidity, which, of course, must be treasured. For the past three months now I have been in and out of the hospital, with days marked by lengthy and painful treatments, blood transfusions, endless tests, hours and hours of unproductive time spent staring at the ceiling, draining fatigue and infection, inability to do normal work, and thinking, thinking, thinking.

But there are also the intermittent passages of lucidity and reflection that sometimes give the mind a perspective on daily life that allows it to see things (without being able to do much about them) from a different perspective. Reading the news from Palestine and seeing the frightful images of death and destruction on television, it has been my experience to be utterly amazed and aghast at what I have deduced from those details about Israeli government policy, more particularly about what has been going on in the mind of Ariel Sharon. And when, after the recent Gaza bombing by one of his F-16s in which nine children were massacred, he was quoted as congratulating the pilot and boasting of a great Israeli success, I was able to form a much clearer idea than before of what a pathologically deranged mind is capable of, not only in terms of what it plans and orders but, worse, how it manages to persuade other minds to think in the same delusional and criminal way. Getting inside the official Israeli mind is a worthwhile, if lurid, experience.

In the West, however, there's been such repetitious and unedifying attention paid to Palestinian suicide bombing that a gross distortion in reality has completely obscured what is much worse: the official Israeli, and perhaps the uniquely Sharonian evil that has been visited so deliberately and so methodically on the Palestinian people. Suicide bombing is reprehensible but it is a direct and, in my opinion, a consciously programmed result of years of abuse, powerlessness and despair. It has as little to do with the Arab or Muslim supposed propensity for violence as the man in the moon. Sharon wants terrorism, not peace, and he does everything in his power to create the conditions for it. But for all its horror, Palestinian violence, the response of a desperate and horribly oppressed people, has been stripped of its context and the terrible suffering from which it arises: a failure to see that is a failure in humanity, and that context doesn't make the violence any less terrible but at least situates it in a real history and real geography.

Yet the location of Palestinian terror—of course it is terror—is never allowed a moment's chance to appear, so remorseless has been the focus on it as a phenomenon apart, a pure, gratuitous evil which Israel, supposedly acting on behalf of pure good, has been virtuously battling in its variously appalling acts of disproportionate violence against a population of three million Palestinian civilians. I am not speaking only about Israel's manipulation of opinion, but its exploitation of the American equivalent of the campaign against terrorism without which Israel could not have done what it has done. (In fact, I cannot think of any other country on earth that, in full view of nightly TV audiences, has performed such miracles of detailed sadism against an entire society and gotten away with it.) That this evil has been made consciously part of George W. Bush's campaign against terrorism, irrationally magnifying American fantasies and fixations with extraordinary ease, is no small part of its blind destructiveness. Like the brigades of eager (and in my opinion completely corrupt) American intellectuals who spin enormous structures of falsehoods about the benign purpose and necessity of US imperialism, Israeli society has pressed into service numerous academics, policy intellectuals at think tanks, and ex-military men now in defense-related and public relations business, all to rationalize and make convincing inhuman punitive policies that are supposedly based on the need for Israeli security.

Israeli security is now a fabled beast. Like a unicorn it is endlessly hunted and never found, remaining, everlastingly, the goal of future action. That over time Israel has become less secure and more unacceptable to its neighbors scarcely merits a moment's notice. But then who challenges the view that Israeli security ought to define the moral world we live in? Certainly not the Arab and Palestinian leaderships, who for 30 years have conceded everything to Israeli security. Shouldn't that ever be questioned, given that Israel has wreaked more damage on the Palestinians and other Arabs relative to its size than any country in the world, Israel with its nuclear arsenal, its air force, navy and army limitlessly supplied by the US taxpayer? As a result the daily, minute occurrences of what Palestinians have to live through are hidden and, more important, covered over by a logic of self-defense and the pursuit of terrorism (terrorist infrastructure, terrorist nests, terrorist bomb factories, terrorist suspects—the list is infinite) which perfectly suits Sharon and the lamentable George Bush. Ideas about terrorism have thus taken on a life of their own, legitimized and re-legitimized without proof, logic or rational argument.

Consider for instance the devastation of Afghanistan, on the one hand, and the "targeted" assassinations of almost 100 Palestinians (to say nothing of the many thousands of "suspects" rounded-up and still imprisoned by Israeli soldiers) on the other: nobody asks whether all these people killed were in fact terrorists, or proved to be terrorists, or were about to become terrorists. They are all assumed to be dangers by acts of simple, unchallenged affirmation. All you need is an arrogant spokesman or two, like the loutish Ranaan Gissin, Avi Pazner or Dore Gold, and in Washington a non-stop apologist for ignorance and incoherence like Ari Fleischer, and the targets in question are just as good as dead. Without doubts, questions or demurral. No need for proof or any such tiresome delicacy. Terrorism and its obsessive pursuit have become an entirely circular, self-fulfilling murder and slow death of enemies who have no choice or say in the matter.

With the exception of reports by a few intrepid journalists and writers such as Amira Hass, Gideon Levy, Amos Elon, Tanya Leibowitz, Jeff Halper, Israel Shamir and a few others, public discourse in the Israeli media has declined terribly in quality and honesty. Patriotism and blind support for the government has replaced skeptical reflection and moral seriousness. Gone are the days of Israel Shahak, Jakob Talmon and Yehoshua Leibowitch. I can think of few Israeli academics and intellectuals—men like Zeev Sternhell, Uri Avnery and Ilan Pappe, for instance—who are courageous enough to depart from the imbecilic and debased debate about "security" and "terrorism" that seems to have overtaken the Israeli peace establishment, or even its rapidly dwindling left opposition. Crimes are being committed every day in the name of Israel and the Jewish people, and yet the intellectuals chatter on about strategic withdrawal, or perhaps whether to incorporate settlements or not, or whether to keep building that monstrous fence (has a crazier idea ever been realized in the modern world, that you can put several million people in a cage and say they don't exist?) in a manner befitting a general or a politician, rather than in ways more suited to intellectuals and artists with independent judgment and some sort of moral standard. Where are the Israeli equivalents of Nadine Gordimer, Andre Brink, Athol Fugard, those white writers who spoke out unequivocally and with unambiguous clarity against the evils of South African apartheid? They simply don't exist in Israel, where public discourse by writers and academics has sunk to equivocation and the repetition of official propaganda, and where most really first-class writing and thought has disappeared from even the academic establishment.

But to return to Israeli practices and the mind-set that has gripped the country with such obduracy during the past few years, think of Sharon's plan. It entails nothing less than the obliteration of an entire people by slow, systematic methods of suffocation, outright murder and the stifling of everyday life. There is a remarkable story by Kafka, *In the Penal Colony,* about a crazed official who shows off a fantastically detailed torture machine whose purpose is to write all over the body of the victim, using a complex apparatus of needles to inscribe the captive's body with minute letters that ultimately causes the prisoner to bleed to death. This is what Sharon and his brigades of willing executioners are doing to the Palestinians, with only the most limited and most symbolic of opposition. Every Palestinian has become a prisoner. Gaza is surrounded by an electrified wire fence on three sides; imprisoned like animals, Gazans are unable to move, unable to work, unable to sell their vegetables or fruit, unable to go to school. They are exposed from the air to Israeli planes and helicopters and are gunned down like turkeys on the ground by tanks and machine guns. Impoverished and starved, Gaza is a human nightmare, each of whose little pieces of episodes—like what takes place at Erez, or near the settlements—involves thousands of soldiers in the humiliation, punishment, intolerable enfeeblement of each Palestinian, without regard for age, gender or illness. Medical supplies are held up at the border, ambulances are fired upon or detained. Hundreds of houses are demolished, and hundreds of thousands of trees and agricultural land destroyed in acts of systematic collective punishment against civilians, most of whom are already refugees from Israel's destruction of their society in 1948. Hope has been eliminated from the Palestinian vocabulary so that only raw defiance remains, and still Sharon and his sadistic minions prattle on about eliminating terrorism by an ever-encroaching occupation that has continued now for 35 years. That the campaign itself is, like all colonial brutality, futile, or that it has the effect of making Palestinians more, rather than less, defiant simply does not enter Sharon's closed mind.

The West Bank is occupied by 1,000 Israeli tanks whose sole purpose is to fire upon and terrorize civilians. Curfews are imposed for periods of up to two weeks, without respite. Schools and universities are either closed or impossible to get to. No one can travel, not just between the nine main cities but within the cities. Every town today is a wasteland of destroyed buildings, looted offices, purposely ruined water and electrical systems. Commerce is finished. Malnutrition prevails in half the number of children. Two-thirds of the population lives below the poverty level of $2 a day. Tanks in Jenin (where the demolition of the refugee camp by Israeli armor, a major war crime, was never investigated because cowardly international bureaucrats such as Kofi Annan back down when Israel threatens) fire upon and kill children, but that is only one drop in an unending stream of Palestinian civilian deaths caused by Israeli soldiers who furnish the illegal Israeli military occupation with loyal, unquestioning service. Palestinians are all "terrorist suspects". The soul of this occupation is that young Israeli conscripts are allowed full rein to subject Palestinians at checkpoints to every known form of private torture and abjection. There is the waiting in the sun for hours; then there is the detention of medical supplies and produce until they rot; there are the insulting words and beatings administered at will; the sudden rampage of jeeps and soldiers against civilians waiting their turn by the thousands at the innumerable checkpoints that have made of Palestinian life a choking hell; making dozens of youths kneel in the sun for hours; forcing men to take off their clothes; insulting and humiliating parents in front of their children; forbidding the sick to pass through for no other reason than personal whim; stopping ambulances and firing on them. And the steady number of Palestinian deaths (quadruple that of Israelis) increases on a daily, mostly untabulated basis. More "terrorist suspects" plus their wives and children, but "we" regret those deaths very much. Thank you.

Israel is frequently referred to as a democracy. If so, then it is a democracy without a conscience, a country whose soul has been captured by a mania for punishing the weak, a democracy that faithfully mirrors the psychopathic mentality of its ruler, General Sharon, whose sole idea—if that is the right word for it— is to kill, reduce, maim, drive away Palestinians until "they break". He provides nothing more concrete as a goal for his campaigns, now or in the past, beyond that, and like the garrulous official in Kafka's story he is most proud of his machine for abusing defenseless Palestinian civilians, all the while monstrously abetted in his grotesque lies by his court advisers and philosophers and generals, as well as by his chorus of faithful American servants. There is no Palestinian army of occupation, no Palestinian tanks, no soldiers, no helicopter gun-ships, no artillery, no government to speak of. But there are the "terrorists" and the "violence" that Israel has invented so that its own neuroses can be inscribed on the bodies of Palestinians, without effective protest from the overwhelming majority of Israel's laggard philosophers, intellectuals, artists, peace activists. Palestinian schools, libraries and universities have ceased normal functioning for months now; and we still wait for the Western freedom-to-write groups and the vociferous defenders of academic freedom in America to raise their voices in protest. I have yet to see one academic organization either in Israel or in the West make a declaration about this profound abrogation of the Palestinian right to knowledge, to learning, to attend school.

In sum, Palestinians must die a slow death so that Israel can have its security, which is just around the corner but cannot be realized because of the special Israeli "insecurity". The whole world must sympathize, while the cries of Palestinian orphans, sick old women, bereaved communities and tortured prisoners simply go unheard and unrecorded. Doubtless, we will be told, these horrors serve a larger purpose than mere sadistic cruelty. After all, "the two sides" are engaged in a "cycle of violence" which has to be stopped, sometime, somewhere. Once in a while, we ought to pause and declare indignantly that there is only one side with an army and a country: the other is a stateless, dispossessed population without rights or any present way of securing them. The language of suffering and concrete daily life has either been hijacked, or it has been so perverted as, in my opinion, to be useless except as pure fiction deployed as a screen for the purpose of more killing and painstaking torture—slowly, fastidiously, inexorably. That is the truth of what Palestinians suffer. But in any case, Israeli policy will ultimately fail.

ANYONE WHO BELIEVES THAT THE ROAD MAP DEVISED BY THE Bush administration actually offers anything resembling a settlement or that it tackles the basic issues is wrong. Like so much of the prevailing peace discourse, it places the need for restraint and renunciation and sacrifice squarely on Palestinian shoulders, thus denying the density and sheer gravity of Palestinian history. To read through the road map is to confront an unsituated document, oblivious of its time and place.

The road map, in other words, is not about a plan for peace so much as a plan for pacification: it is about putting an end to Palestine as a problem. Hence the repetition of the term "performance" in the document's wooden prose—in other words, how the Palestinians are expected to behave, almost in the social sense of the word. No violence, no protest, more democracy, better leaders and institutions, all based on the notion that the underlying problem has been the ferocity of Palestinian resistance, rather than the occupation that has given rise to it.

Nothing comparable is expected of Israel except that a few small settlements, known as "illegal outposts" (an entirely new classification which suggests that some Israeli implantations on Palestinian land are legal) must be given up and, yes, the major settlements "frozen" but certainly not dismantled. Not a word is said about what since 1948, and then again since 1967, Palestinians have endured at the hands of Israel and the US. Nothing about the de-development of the Palestinian economy as described by the American researcher Sara Roy in her forthcoming *Scholarship and Politics*. House demolitions, the uprooting of trees, the 5000 prisoners or more, the policy of targeted assassinations, the closures since 1993, the wholesale ruin of the infrastructure, the incredible number of deaths and maimings— all that and more passes without a word.

Nonetheless ... It may seem quixotic for me to say, even if the immediate prospects are grim from a Palestinian perspective, they are not all dark. The Palestinians stubbornly survive, and Palestinian society—devastated, nearly ruined, desolate in so many ways—is, like Hardy's thrush in its blast-beruffled plume, still capable of flinging its soul upon the growing gloom. No other Arab society is as rambunctious and healthily unruly, and none is fuller of civic and social initiatives and functioning institutions (including a miraculously vital musical conservatory). Even though they are mostly unorganized and in some cases lead miserable lives of exile and statelessness, Diaspora Palestinians are still energetically engaged by the problems of their collective destiny, and everyone that I know is always trying somehow to advance the cause. Only a minuscule fraction of this energy has ever found its way into the Palestinian Authority, which except for the highly ambivalent figure of Arafat has remained strangely marginal to the common fate. According to recent polls, [in the early summer of 2003] Fateh and Hamas between them have the support of roughly 45 percent of the Palestinian electorate, with the remaining

55 percent evolving quite different, much more hopeful-looking political formations.

One in particular has struck me as significant (and I have attached myself to it) inasmuch as it now provides the only genuine grassroots formation that steers clear both of the religious parties and their fundamentally sectarian politics, and of the traditional nationalism offered up by Arafat's old (rather than young) Fateh activists. It's been called the National Political Initiative (NPI) and its main figure is Mostapha Barghuti, a Moscow-trained physician, whose main work has been as director of the impressive Village Medical Relief Committee, which has brought health care to more than 100,000 rural Palestinians. A former Communist Party stalwart, Barghuti is a quiet-spoken organizer and leader who has overcome the hundreds of physical obstacles impeding Palestinian movement or travel abroad to rally nearly every independent individual and organization of note behind a political program that promises social reform as well as liberation across doctrinal lines. Singularly free of conventional rhetoric, Barghuti has worked with Israelis, Europeans, Americans, Africans, Asians, Arabs to build an enviably well-run solidarity movement that practices the pluralism and co-existence it preaches. NPI does not throw up its hands at the directionless militarization of the intifada. It offers training programs for the unemployed and social services for the destitute on the grounds that this answers to present circumstances and Israeli pressure. Above all, NPI, which is about to become a recognized political party, seeks to mobilize Palestinian society at home and in exile for free elections—authentic elections which will represent Palestinian, rather than Israeli or US, interests. This sense of authenticity is what seems so lacking in the path cut out for Abu Mazen.

The vision here isn't a manufactured provisional state on 40 percent of the land, with the refugees abandoned and Jerusalem kept by Israel, but a sovereign territory liberated from military occupation by mass action involving Arabs and Jews wherever possible. Because NPI is an authentic Palestinian movement, reform and democracy have become part of its everyday practice. Many hundreds of Palestine's most notable activists and independents have already signed up, and organizational meetings have already been held, with many more planned abroad and in Palestine, despite the terrible difficulties of getting around Israel's restrictions on freedom of movement. It is some solace to think that, while formal negotiations and discussions go on, a host of informal, un-coopted alternatives exist, of which NPI and a growing international solidarity campaign are now the main components.

IN EARLY MAY, I WAS IN SEATTLE LECTURING FOR A FEW DAYS. While there, I had dinner one night with Rachel Corrie's parents and sister, who were still reeling from the shock of their daughter's murder on March 16 in Gaza by an Israeli bulldozer. Mr. Corrie told me that he had himself driven bulldozers, although the one that killed his daughter deliberately because she was trying valiantly to protect a Palestinian home in Rafah from demolition was a 60 ton behemoth especially designed by Caterpillar for house demolitions, a far bigger machine than anything he had ever seen or driven. Two things struck me about my brief visit with the Corries. One was the story they told about their return to the US with their daughter's body. They had immediately sought out their US senators, Patty Murray and Maria Cantwell, both Democrats, told them their story and received the expected expressions of shock, outrage, anger and promises of investigations. After both women returned to Washington, the Corries never heard from them again, and the promised investigation simply didn't materialize. As expected, the Israel lobby had explained the realities to them, and both women simply begged off. An American citizen willfully murdered by the soldiers of a client state of the US without so much as an official peep or even the de rigeur investigation that had been promised her family.

But the second and far more important aspect of the Rachel Corrie story for me was the young woman's action itself, heroic and dignified at the same time. Born and brought up in Olympia, a small city 60 miles south of Seattle, she had joined the International Solidarity Movement and gone to Gaza to stand with suffering human beings with whom she had never had any contact before. Her letters back to her family are truly remarkable documents of her ordinary humanity that make for very difficult and moving reading, especially when she describes the kindness and concern showed her by all the Palestinians she encounters who clearly welcome her as one of their own, because she lives with them exactly as they do, sharing their lives and worries, as well as the horrors of the Israeli occupation and its terrible effects on even the smallest child. She understands the fate of refugees, and what she calls the Israeli government's insidious attempt at a kind of genocide by making it almost impossible for this particular group of people to survive. So moving is her solidarity that it inspires an Israeli reservist named Danny who has refused service to write her and tell her, "You are doing a good thing. I thank you for it."

What shines through all the letters she wrote home, which were subsequently published in the London Guardian, is the amazing resistance put up by the Palestinian people themselves, average human beings stuck in the most terrible position of suffering and despair but continuing to survive just the same. We have heard so much recently about the road map and the prospects for peace that we have overlooked the most basic fact of all, which is that Palestinians have refused to capitulate or surrender even under the collective punishment meted out to them by the combined might of the US and Israel. It is that extraordinary fact that is the reason for the existence of a road map and all the numerous so-called peace plans before it, not at all some conviction on the part of the US and Israel and the international community for humanitarian reasons that the killing and the violence must stop. If we miss that truth about the power of Palestinian resistance (by which I do not at all mean suicide bombing, which does much more harm than good), despite all its failings and all its mistakes, we miss everything. Palestinians have always been a problem for the Zionist project, and so-called solutions have perennially been proposed that minimize, rather than solve, the problem. The official Israeli policy, no matter whether Ariel Sharon uses the word "occupation" or not or whether or not he dismantles a rusty, unused tower or two, has always been not to accept the reality of the Palestinian people as equals or ever to admit that their rights were scandalously violated all along by Israel. Whereas a few courageous Israelis over the years have tried to deal with this other concealed history, most Israelis and what seems like the majority of American Jews have made every effort to deny, avoid, or negate the Palestinian reality. This is why there is no peace. Moreover, the road map says nothing about justice or about the historical punishment meted out to the Palestinian people for too many decades to count. What Rachel Corrie's work in Gaza recognized, however, was precisely the gravity and the density of the living history of the Palestinian people as a national community, and not merely as a collection of deprived refugees. That is what she was in solidarity with. And we need to remember that that kind of solidarity is no longer confined to a small number of intrepid souls here and there, but is recognized the world over. In the past six months I have lectured in four continents to many thousands of people. What brings them together is Palestine and the struggle of the Palestinian people which is now a byword for emancipation and enlightenment, regardless of all the vilification heaped on them by their enemies.

Whenever the facts are made known, there is immediate recognition and an expression of the most profound solidarity

with the justice of the Palestinian cause and the valiant struggle
by the Palestinian people on its behalf. It is an extraordinary
thing that Palestine was a central issue this year both during the
Porto Alegre anti-globalization meetings as well as during the
Davos and Amman meetings, both poles of the world-wide political spectrum. Simply because our fellow citizens in this country
are fed an atrociously biased diet of ignorance and misrepresen-
tation by the media, where the occupation is never referred to in
lurid descriptions of suicide attacks, where the apartheid wall 25
feet high, five feet thick and 350 kilometers long that Israel is
building is never even shown on the networks (or so much as
referred to in passing throughout the lifeless prose of the road
map), and where the crimes of war, the gratuitous destruction
and humiliation, maiming and death imposed on Palestinian
civilians are never shown for the daily, completely routine ordeal
that they are, one shouldn't be surprised that Americans in the
main have a very low opinion of Arabs and Palestinians. After
all, please remember that all the main organs of the establishment media, from left liberal all the way over to fringe right, are
unanimously anti-Arab, anti-Muslim and anti-Palestinian. Look
at the pusillanimity of the media during the buildup to an illegal
and unjust war against Iraq, and look at how little coverage there
was of the immense damage against Iraqi society done by the
sanctions, and how relatively few accounts there were of the
immense world-wide outpouring of opinion against the war.
Hardly a single journalist except Helen Thomas took the administration directly to task for the outrageous lies and confected
"facts" that were spun out about Iraq as an imminent military
threat to the US before the war, just as now the same government propagandists who cynically invented and manipulated
"facts" about WMD are let off the hook by media heavies in dis-
cussing the awful, the literally inexcusable situation for the
people of Iraq that the US has irresponsibly and almost single-
handedly created there. However else one blames Saddam

Hussein as a vicious tyrant, which he was, he had provided the people of Iraq with the best infrastructure of services like water, electricity, health and education of any Arab country. None of this is any longer in place.

With the extraordinary fear of seeming anti-Semitic by criticizing Israel for its daily crimes of war against innocent, unarmed Palestinian civilians, or seeming anti-American for criticizing the US government for its illegal war and its dreadfully run military occupation, it is no wonder, then, that the vicious media and government campaign against Arab society, culture, history and mentality that has been led by Neanderthal publicists and Orientalists like Bernard Lewis and Daniel Pipes has cowed far too many of us into believing that Arabs really are an underdeveloped, incompetent and doomed people, and that with all the failures in democracy and development, Arabs are alone in this world for being retarded, behind the times, unmodernized and deeply reactionary. Here is where dignity and critical historical thinking must be mobilized to see what is what and to disentangle truth from propaganda.

No one would deny that most Arab countries today are ruled by unpopular regimes and that vast numbers of poor, disadvantaged young Arabs are exposed to the ruthless forms of fundamentalist religion. Yet it is simply a lie to say, as The New York Times regularly does, that Arab societies are totally controlled, and that there is no freedom of opinion, no civil institutions, no functioning social movements for and by the people. Press laws notwithstanding, you can go to downtown Amman today and buy a Communist Party newspaper as well as an Islamist one; Egypt and Lebanon are full of papers and journals that suggest much more debate and discussion than these societies are given credit for; the satellite channels are bursting with opinions of a dizzying variety; civil institutions are, on many levels having to do with social services, human rights, syndicates and research institutes, very lively all over the Arab world. A great deal more must be done before we have the appropriate level of democracy, but we are on the way.

In Palestine alone there are over 1000 NGO's and it is this vitality and this kind of activity that has kept society going. Under the worst possible circumstances, Palestinian society has neither been defeated nor has it crumbled completely. Kids still go to school, doctors and nurses still take care of their patients, men and women go to work, organizations have their meetings, and people continue to live, which seems to be an offense to Sharon and the other extremists who simply want Palestinians either imprisoned or driven away altogether. The military solution hasn't worked at all, and never will work. Why is that so hard for Israelis to see? We must help them to understand this, not by suicide bombs but by rational argument, mass civil disobedience, organized protest, here and everywhere.

The point I am trying to make is that we have to see the Arab world generally and Palestine in particular in more comparative and critical ways than superficial and dismissive books like Lewis's What Went Wrong and Paul Wolfowitz's ignorant statements about bringing democracy to the Arab and Islamic world even begin to suggest. Whatever else is true about the Arabs, there is an active dynamic at work because as real people they live in a real society with all sorts of currents and crosscurrents which can't be easily caricatured as just one seething mass of violent fanaticism. The Palestinian struggle for justice is especially something with which one must express solidarity, rather than endless criticism and exasperated, frustrating discouragement, or crippling divisiveness. Remember the solidarity here and everywhere in Latin America, Africa, Europe, Asia and Australia, and remember also that there is a cause to which many people have committed themselves, difficulties and terrible obstacles notwithstanding. Why? Because it is a just cause, a noble ideal, a moral quest for equality and human rights.

I want now to speak about dignity, which of course has a special place in every culture known to historians, anthropologists, sociologists and humanists. I shall begin by saying immediately that it is a radically wrong, Orientalist and indeed racist proposition to accept that, unlike Europeans and Americans, Arabs have no sense of individuality, no regard for individual life, no values that express love, intimacy and understanding which are supposed to be the property exclusively of cultures that had a Renaissance, a Reformation and an Enlightenment. Among many others, it is the vulgar and jejune Thomas Friedman who has been peddling this rubbish, which has alas been picked up by equally ignorant and self-deceiving Arab intellectuals—I don't need to mention any names here—who have seen in the atrocities of 9/11 a sign that the Arab and Islamic worlds are somehow more diseased and more dysfunctional than any other, and that terrorism is a sign of a wider distortion than has occurred in any other culture.

We can leave to one side that, between them, Europe and the US account for by far the largest number of violent deaths during the 20th century, the Islamic world hardly a fraction of it. Behind all of that specious, unscientific nonsense about wrong and right civilizations, there is the grotesque shadow of the great false prophet Samuel Huntington, who has led a lot of people to believe that the world can be divided into distinct civilizations battling against each other forever. But Huntington is dead wrong on every point he makes. No culture or civilization exists by itself; none is made up of things like individuality and enlightenment that are exclusive to it; and none exists without the basic human attributes of community, love, value for life and all the others. To suggest otherwise as he does is the purest invidious racism of the same stripe as that of people who argue that Africans have naturally inferior brains, or that Asians are really born for servitude, or that Europeans are a naturally superior race. This is a sort of parody of Hitlerian science directed uniquely today against Arabs and Muslims, and we must be very firm as to not even go through the motions of arguing against it. It is the purest drivel. On the other hand, there is the much more credible and serious stipulation that, like every other instance of humanity, Arab and Muslim life has an inherent value and dignity that are expressed by Arabs and Muslims in their unique cultural style, and those expressions needn't resemble or be a copy of one approved model suitable for everyone to follow.

The whole point about human diversity is that it is in the end a form of deep co-existence between very different styles of individuality and experience that can't all be reduced to one superior form: this is the spurious argument foisted on us by pundits who bewail the lack of development and knowledge in the Arab world. All one has to do is to look at the huge variety of literature, cinema, theater, painting, music and popular culture produced by and for Arabs from Morocco to the Gulf. Surely that needs to be assessed as an indication of whether or not Arabs are developed, and not just how on any given day statistical tables of industrial production either indicate an appropriate level of development or show failure.

The more important point I want to make, though, is that there is a very wide discrepancy today between our cultures and societies and the small group of people who now rule these societies. Rarely in history has such power been so concentrated in so tiny a group as the various kings, generals, sultans and presidents who preside today over the Arabs. The worst thing about them as a group, almost without exception, is that they do not represent the best of their people. This is not just a matter of no democracy. It is that they seem to radically underestimate themselves and their people in ways that close them off, that make them intolerant and fearful of change, frightened of opening up their societies to their people, terrified most of all that they might anger big brother, that is, the United States. Instead of seeing their citizens as the potential wealth of the nation, they regard them all as guilty conspirators vying for the ruler's power.

This is the real failure, how during the terrible war against the Iraqi people, no Arab leader had the self-dignity and confidence to say something about the pillaging and military occupation of one of the most important Arab countries. Fine, it is an excellent thing that Saddam Hussein's appalling regime is no more, but who appointed the US to be the Arab mentor? Who asked the US to take over the Arab world allegedly on behalf of its citizens and bring it something called "democracy", especially at a time when the school system, the health system and the whole economy in America are degenerating to the worst levels since the 1929 Depression? Why was the collective Arab voice NOT raised against the US's flagrantly illegal intervention, which did so much harm and inflicted so much humiliation upon the entire Arab nation? This is truly a colossal failure in nerve, in dignity, in self-solidarity.

With all the Bush administration's talk about guidance from the Almighty, doesn't one Arab leader have the courage just to say that, as a great people, we are guided by our own lights and traditions and religions? But nothing, not a word, as the poor citizens of Iraq live through the most terrible ordeals and the rest of the region quakes in its collective boots, each one petrified that his country may be next. How unfortunate the embrace of George Bush, the man whose war destroyed an Arab country gratuitously, by the combined leadership of the major Arab countries. Was there no one who had the guts to remind George W. that he has brought more suffering to the Arab people than anyone before him? Must he always be greeted with hugs, smiles, kisses and low bows? Where is the diplomatic and political and economic support necessary to sustain an anti-occupation movement on the West Bank and Gaza? Instead all one hears is foreign ministers preaching to the Palestinians to mind their ways, avoid violence and keep at the peace negotiations, even though it has been so obvious that Sharon's interest in peace is just about zero. There has been no concerted Arab response to the separation wall, or to the assassinations, or to collective punishment, only a bunch of tired clichés repeating the well-worn formulas authorized by the State Department.

Perhaps the one thing that strikes me as the low point in Arab inability to grasp the dignity of the Palestinian cause is expressed by the current state of the Palestinian Authority. Abu Mazen, a subordinate figure with little political support among his own people, was picked for the job by Arafat, Israel and the US precisely because he has no constituency, is not an orator or a great organizer, or anything really except a dutiful aide to Yasser Arafat, and because I am afraid they see in him a man who will do Israel's bidding. How could even Abu Mazen stand there in Aqaba to pronounce words written for him, like a ventriloquist's puppet, by some State Department functionary, in which he commendably speaks about Jewish suffering but then amazingly says next to nothing about his own people's suffering at the hands of Israel? How could he accept so undignified and manipulated a role for himself, and how could he forget his self-respect as the representative of a people that has been fighting heroically for its rights for over a century just because the US and Israel have told him he must? And when Israel simply says that there will be a "provisional" Palestinian state, without any contrition for the horrendous amount of damage it has done, the uncountable war crimes, the sheer sadistic, systematic humiliation of every single Palestinian, man, woman, child, I must confess to a complete lack of understanding as to why a leader or representative of that people doesn't so much as take note of it. Has he entirely lost his sense of dignity?

Has he forgotten that he is not just an individual but also the bearer of his people's fate at an especially crucial moment? Is there anyone who was not bitterly disappointed at this total failure to rise to the occasion and stand with dignity—the dignity of his people's experience and cause—and testify to it with pride, and without compromise, without ambiguity, without the half embarrassed, half apologetic tone that Palestinian leaders take when they are begging for a little kindness from some totally unworthy white father?

But that has been the behavior of Palestinian rulers since Oslo and indeed since Haj Amin, a combination of misplaced juvenile defiance and plaintive supplication. Why on earth do they always think it absolutely necessary to read scripts written for them by their enemies? The basic dignity of our life as Arabs in Palestine, throughout the Arab world, and here in America, is that we are our own people, with a heritage, a history, a tradition and above all a language that is more than adequate to the task of representing our real aspirations, since those aspirations derive from the experience of dispossession and suffering that has been imposed on each Palestinian since 1948. Not one of our political spokespeople—the same is true of the Arabs since Abdel Nasser's time—ever speaks with self-respect and dignity of what we are, what we want, what we have done and where we want to go.

Slowly, however, the situation is changing, and the old regime made up of the Abu Mazens and Abu Ammars of this world is passing and will gradually be replaced by a new set of emerging leaders all over the Arab world. The most promising is made up of the members of the National Political Initiative; they are grassroots activists whose main activity is not pushing papers on a desk, nor juggling bank accounts, nor looking for journalists to pay attention to them, but who come from the ranks of the professionals, the working classes, the young intellectuals and activists, the teachers, doctors, lawyers, working people who have kept society going while also fending off daily Israeli attacks. Second, these are people committed to the kind of democracy and popular participation undreamt of by the Authority, whose idea of democracy is stability and security for itself. Lastly, they offer social services to the unemployed, health to the uninsured and the poor, proper secular education to a new generation of Palestinians who must be taught the realities of the modern world, not just the extraordinary worth of the old one. For such programs, the NPI stipulates that getting rid of the occupation is the only way forward, and that in order to do that, a representative national unified leadership must be elected freely to replace the cronies, the outdated perspectives and the ineffectiveness that have plagued Palestinian leaders for the past century.

Only if we respect ourselves as Arabs and understand the true dignity and justice of our struggle, only then can we appreciate why, almost despite ourselves, so many people all over the world, including Rachel Corrie and the two young people wounded with her from ISM, Tom Hurndall and Brian Avery, have felt it possible to express their solidarity with us.

I conclude with one last irony. Isn't it astonishing that all the signs of popular solidarity that Palestine and the Arabs receive occur with no comparable sign of solidarity and dignity for ourselves, that others admire and respect us more than we do ourselves? Isn't it time we caught up with our own status and made certain that our representatives here and elsewhere realize, as a first step, that they are fighting for a just and noble cause, and that they have nothing to apologize for or anything to be embarrassed about? On the contrary, they should be proud of what their people have done and proud also to represent them.

Edward Said is a Professor of Literature at Columbia University. His latest book is Freud and the Non-Europeans.

Index

AK Press

Ordering Information

AK Press
674-A 23rd Street
Oakland, CA 94612-1163
USA
(510) 208-1700
www.akpress.org
akpress@akpress.org

AK Press
PO Box 12766
Edinburgh, EH8 9YE
Scotland
(0131) 555-5165
www.akuk.com
ak@akedin.demon.uk

The addresses above would be delighted to provide you with the latest complete AK catalog, featuring several thousand books, pamphlets, zines, audio products, video products, and stylish apparel published & distributed by AK Press. Alternatively, check out our websites for the complete catalog, latest news and updates, events, and secure ordering.

Also Available from AK Press

The first audio collection from Alexander Cockburn on compact disc.

Beating the Devil

Alexander Cockburn, ISBN: 1 902593 49 9   ●   CD   ● $14.98

In this collection of recent talks, maverick commentator Alexander Cockburn defiles subjects ranging from Colombia to the American presidency to the Missile Defense System. Whether he's skewering the fallacies of the war on drugs or illuminating the dark crevices of secret government, his erudite and extemporaneous style warms the hearts of even the stodgiest cynics of the left.

Next from CounterPunch/AK Press

Coming in 2004

Serpents in The Garden: Liaisons with Culture and Sex

Edited by Alexander Cockburn and Jeffrey St. Clair

A spring collection of vivacious essays on the politics of art, music, architecture and sex. In addition to more than a dozen stories by Cockburn and St. Clair, there's a score of other radical tilts by the country's wildest CounterPunchers.

A Dime's Worth of Difference? Beyond the Lesser of Two Evils

Edited by Alexander Cockburn and Jeffrey St. Clair

Cockburn and St. Clair, authors of the classic 2000 take-down, *Al Gore: A User's Manual* (also available from CounterPunch) conduct a teach-in on the candidates, the issues and what's really at stake.

Also Available from CounterPunch and AK Press, (call 1-800-840-3683 or order online at www.akpress.org)

Whiteout: the CIA, Drugs and the Press

by Alexander Cockburn and Jeffrey St. Clair, VERSO.

The involvement of the CIA with drug traffickers is a story that has slouched into the limelight every decade or so since the creation of the Agency. In Whiteout, here at last is the full saga.

Been Brown So Long It Looked Like Green to Me: the Politics of Nature

by Jeffrey St. Clair, COMMON COURAGE PRESS.

Covering everything from toxics to electric power plays, St. Clair draws a savage profile of how money and power determine the state of our environment, gives a vivid account of where the environment stands today and what to do about it.

The Golden Age Is In Us

by Alexander Cockburn, VERSO.

Cockburn's classic diary of the late 80s and early 90s.

"A Patchwork Paradise Lost", Times Literary Supplement.

"A literary gem", Village Voice.

Why We Publish CounterPunch
By Alexander Cockburn and Jeffrey St. Clair

Ten years ago we felt unhappy about the state of radical journalism. It didn't have much edge. It didn't have many facts. It was politically timid. It was dull. CounterPunch was founded. We wanted it to be the best muckraking newsletter in the country. We wanted it to take aim at the consensus of received wisdom about what can and cannot be reported. We wanted to give our readers a political roadmap they could trust.

A decade later we stand firm on these same beliefs and hopes. We think we've restored honor to muckraking journalism in the tradition of our favorite radical pamphleteers: Edward Abbey, Peter Maurin and Ammon Hennacy, Appeal to Reason, Jacques René Hébert, Tom Paine and John Lilburne.

Every two weeks CounterPunch gives you jaw-dropping exposés on: Congress and lobbyists; the environment; labor; the National Security State.

"CounterPunch kicks through the floorboards of lies and gets to the foundation of what is really going on in this country", says Michael Ratner, attorney at the Center for Constitutional Rights. "At our house, we fight over who gets to read CounterPunch first. Each issue is like spring after a cold, dark winter."

YOU CANNOT MISS ANOTHER ISSUE

Name _____

Address _____

City _____ State _____ Zip _____

Email _____ Phone _____

Credit Card # _____

Exp. Date _____ Signature _____

Visit our website for more information: **www.counterpunch.org**

☐ 1 yr. **$40**   ☐ 1 yr. email **$35**   ☐ 1 yr. both **$45**

☐ 2 yr. **$70**   ☐ 2 yr. email **$60**   ☐ 2 yr. both **$80**

☐ 1 yr. low income **$30**   ☐ 2 yr. low income **$65**

☐ Supporter **$100**   ☐ Donation Only

Send Check/Money Order to: **CounterPunch, P.O. Box 228, Petrolia, CA 95558**
Canada add $12.50 per year postage. Others outside US add $17.50 per year.